BECOMING THE LORD'S SHOFAR

The Process of Transformation

Dr. Michael H Yeager

Cover is a painting by

Kathy Berry

http://www.kathyberryillustrations.com/shop/the-prophet

ISBN 9781542855198

Create Space Independent Publishing Platform

(Some of the information in this book is partly taken from the Adam Clarke Commentary, and other non-copy right material found on the internet)

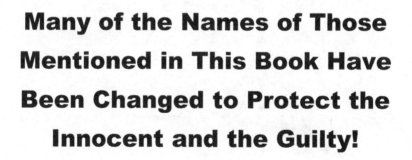

Many of the Names of Those Mentioned in This Book Have Been Changed to Protect the Innocent and the Guilty!

DEDICATION

We dedicate this book to those who are truly hungry and thirsty to live in the realm of the supernatural, and to those who have already tasted of the heavenly realm. We dedicate this to the bride of Christ, those who are called to go deeper, higher, and farther than they have yet experienced. It is only by the grace that comes by FAITH in CHRIST that we will be able to accomplish His will in this earth.

Introduction

A vision of the **SHOFAR** - I had an open vision, I saw a RAM'S **HORN** which had not yet been converted to a **SHOFAR**. It was twisted, covered with thick ridges and bumps. It was an ugly long ram's **HORN**.

Right before my eyes, there appeared to the right of this **HORN** another **HORN**. I knew within my heart it was the same **HORN** that had gone through a Divine process. It was an incredible transformation. The old nature, the old flesh, the old ways had been removed.

There now ran a Holy air vent all the way through this transformed RAM'S **HORN**. It was no longer a dead, lifeless, useless **HORN**, but it had become a sacred Instrument to be used in the Divine plans and purposes of **God**. It had become A Holy **SHOFAR**! This book is all about that process that a Believer MUST go through to be used of **GOD** in Amazing and Supernatural ways!

GOD Said: You Better Not Lie or You'll Die!

One day in 1979, I picked up a book by a well-known author. This book had come highly recommended by one of my favorite preachers at that time. The topic was about angelic visitations. This was something I was interested in, because of my many experiences with the supernatural. I began to read this book and noticed immediately that there were experiences he said he had, which did not seem to line up with the Scriptures. I did not want to judge his heart, but we do have the responsibility to examine everything in light of **God**'s Word. If it does not line up with the word of **God**, then we must reject it, no matter who wrote it.

As I was pondering the stories in this book, the **Spirit** of the Lord spoke to my heart very strongly. It was as if He was standing right there next to me, speaking audibly. What He spoke to me was rather shocking! The Lord told me that the writer of this book would be dead in three months from a heart attack. I asked the Lord why He was telling me this. He said the stories in the man's book were exaggerated, and that he had opened the door for the devil to steal his life. The Lord warned me that day that if I were ever to do the same thing, judgment would come to me. I did not realize that the Lord would have me to be writing books; many of them filled with my own experiences. Now I know why he spoke this to me, telling me that I better not exaggerate my experiences.

When the **Spirit** of the Lord spoke this to me, I turned and told my wife. I held the book up and said, in a very quiet whispering, trembling, wavering **Voice**, "Honey, the man who wrote this book will be dead in three months from a heart attack." Plus, I told her why the Lord told me this. I wish I had been wrong.

Exactly three months later, the man died from a heart attack. **God** can speak to us through the positive and the negative circumstances of life. We better take heed to what he is saying.

2 Timothy 2:19 Nevertheless, the foundation of God standeth sure, having this seal, The Lord knoweth them that are his. And, Let every one that nameth the name of Christ depart from iniquity. 20 But in a great house, there are not only vessels of gold and of silver, but also of wood and of earth; and some to honor, and some to dishonor. 21 If a man, therefore, purge himself from these, he shall be a vessel unto honor, sanctified, and meet for the Master's use, and prepared unto every good work.

CONTENTS

ACKNOWLEDGMENTS

*To our heavenly Father and His wonderful love.

*To our Lord, Savior, and Master — Jesus Christ, Who saved us and set us free because of His great love for us.

*To the Holy Spirit, Who leads and guides us into the realm of truth and miraculous living every day.

*Thanks to all of those who had a part in helping me get this book ready for publishing.

*To my Lovely Wife, and our precious children, Michael, Daniel, Steven, Stephanie, Catherine Yu, who is our precious daughter-in-law, and Naomi, who is now with the Lord.

CHAPTER ONE

The TRUMPET of God

SHOFAR

Typical Ashkenazi SHOFAR from a ram's HORN
A SHOFAR (IPA: [ˈʃoʊfər]—Heb: שופר) is a HORN that is used as a musical instrument for Jewish religious purposes.

In biblical times the SHOFAR was used as a signaling device in time of war, most famously at the Battle of Jericho. It later served as an accompanying instrument for the performance of psalms in the Temple of Jerusalem. Since the destruction of the Temple in 70 C.E., it has played a more restricted role in Jewish religious life.

The method of playing the SHOFAR is similar to that of bugle, with pitch variations created by adjusting the lips while blowing. The SHOFAR is usually constructed from a ram's HORN, although the HORNs of many other animals are also accepted. It is considered an instrument for sacred use, and the manner of playing it is closely prescribed in Jewish tradition.

SHOFARs in the Bible

Priests blow SHOFARs in preparation for the attack on Jericho.
The SHOFAR, usually translated as "TRUMPET," is mentioned frequently in the Hebrew Bible and throughout the Talmud and later rabbinic literature.

In the story of the Exodus, it was the Voice of the divine SHOFAR, "exceeding loud," that issued from the thick cloud on Mount Sinai and made all the Israelites tremble in awe:

On the morning of the third day, there was THUNDER and lightning, with a thick cloud over the mountain, and an exceedingly loud TRUMPET blast. Everyone in the camp trembled. Then Moses led the people out of the camp to meet with God, and they stood at the foot of the mountain. Mount Sinai was covered with smoke because the Lord descended on it in FIRE. The smoke billowed up from it like smoke from a furnace, the whole mountain trembled violently, and the sound of the TRUMPET grew louder and

louder. Then Moses spoke, and the Voice of God answered him (Exodus 19:16-19).

The SHOFAR was often taken out to war so the troops would know when a battle would begin (Num. 10:9, Josh. 6:4; Judges 3:27; 7:16, 20; I Sam. 8:3). Most famously, seven SHOFARs were blown in the time of Joshua to help him capture Jericho. As the Israelites surrounded the walls, the SHOFARs were blown by the priests. Finally, the walls collapsed, and the Jews were able to capture the city.

On the seventh day, they got up at daybreak and marched around the city seven times... The seventh time around, when the priests sounded the TRUMPET blast, Joshua commanded the people, "Shout! For the Lord has given you the city! ...At the sound of the TRUMPET, when the people gave a loud shout, the wall collapsed; so every man charged straight in, and they took the city (Josh 6:15-21).

After the conquest of Canaan, the SHOFAR played a prescribed role in Jewish religious life. It was used for the announcement of the new moon and solemn feasts (Num. 10:10; Ps. 81:4), and also for proclaiming the year of jubilee (Lev. 25:9). The first day of the seventh month (Tishri) was termed "a memorial of blowing" the SHOFAR (Lev. 23:24). It was also employed in other religious ceremonials, as in processions (2 Sam. 6. 15; I Chron. 15:28), or in the Temple orchestra as an accompaniment the psalms:

Make music to the Lord with the harp, with the harp and the sound of singing,

with TRUMPETs and the blast of the ram's HORN—shout for joy before the Lord, the King. (Ps. 98:5-6)

On New-Year's Day (Rosh Hashanah) the principal ceremony in the Temple of Jerusalem was conducted with the SHOFAR, which was placed in the center of the orchestra, with a TRUMPET on either side. This SHOFAR was the HORN of a wild goat, straight in shape, and ornamented with gold at the mouthpiece.

On fasting days, the crowning ceremony was conducted with the TRUMPETs in the center and with a SHOFAR on either side. On those occasions, the SHOFARs were rams' HORNs curved in shape and ornamented with silver at the mouthpieces. On Yom Kippur of the jubilee year, the ceremony was performed with the SHOFAR as on New-Year's Day.

According to Maimonides, the SHOFAR message is: "Wake up from your sleep. You are asleep. Get up from your slumber. You are in a deep sleep. Search for your behavior. Become the best person you can. Remember God, the One Who created you."

The Amazing Significance of the SHOFAR (part 1)

In January, Tuesday, the 24th, 2017, I was in prayer in the sanctuary of the church where I pastor. I was approximately into my third hour of an seven-hour prayer time. I was in the word of

God, talking to the Lord, meditating on Scriptures, and singing to **JESUS**, when something supernatural happened. It is not unusual for me to experience supernatural **Visitations**.

The psalmist said: ***As I was musing, the FIRE burned, then spake I with my tongue***. In Ephesians, Paul says that we can be filled with the **Spirit** by speaking to ourselves in Psalms, hymns, and **Spirit**ual songs, singing and making melody in our heart to the Lord. Many people within the body of **CHRIST** never experience **God** manifesting himself to them because they do not give themselves to this type of activity.

As I was ministering to the Lord, I had an open vision. You might ask: what is an **open vision**? In the book of Joel, it is revealed to us that in the last days **God** will give his people dreams and visions. **God** will lead and guide us through Visions. If we went from Genesis to Revelation, we would discover that much of **God**'s will has been revealed to his people by this **Divine** supernatural experience.

The word vision alone appears in the Bible almost 100 times. If you counted every time that **God** gave a vision to one of his people, it would be well into the thousands. This is a major way that **God** reveals HIS will, not just to his people, but to humanity. For instance, **God** called Abraham out of the city of the Chaldean s, and told Abraham his plan and his future, for his life by visions.

Genesis:1 After these things, the word of the Lord came unto Abram in a vision, saying, Fear not, Abram: I am thy shield, and thy exceeding great reward.

I have written several books about visions. Many times my life has been spared because of the visions **God** has given me. I have discovered that there are at least **five different levels of visions**, in which **God** will speak to us and reveal his will. What happened to me on Tuesday is one of the simplest ways in which **God** gives visions. **#1** It is simply a very translucent image or vision that happens in your heart and floats up to your mind! This a very soft and light, sometimes foggy image.

Now, this happens to me all the time. Especially when I go to pray for people, I'll see something going on in someone's life. I'll see a problem, or I'll see a physical disability. Sometimes I'll see something happening in the past or something that is going to happen in the future. Along with most visions, I will also experience a **Divine** download of information that I did not receive from a natural source.

DIVINE DOWNLOADS

Now a **Divine** Download is when **God** supernaturally, instantly puts within our mind and heart information that you have not learned in the natural. We use the terminology "download" with that of a computer. We hook up our computer to the Internet, connect it to a particular link or URL. Then we can download a prog**ram**, a video file, audio file, or download certain information. If you have a high-speed Internet connection, your prog**ram** can download very quickly.

God is the original author of giving people **Divine** downloads. I will provide you with some examples of **God**, giving people **Divine** supernatural downloads in the Bible. When **God** led the children of Israel out of Egypt, all those men and women had been slaves there whole life. In the natural, they probably had very little education. Once they were in the wilderness, **God** went to Moses and told him that he was going to have the people of Israel build a very special and unique Tabernacle, a portable house, where the presence of **God** would abide. If you study this in the book Exodus, you'll discover that this Tabernacle was quite exquisite and complicated.

He told Moses that he was going to supernaturally download this information to the people that he had chosen. The Bible then very explicitly tells us the name of every one of these people, and the supernatural abilities **God** gave them. These people were never trained or taught to work with wood, silver, gold, animal skins, or specialized cloth. And yet here they were with the knowledge, information, and the skills given to them by **God** to perform this unique task of building the tabernacle.

The vision of the SHOFAR

In this open vision, I saw a **RAM**'s **HORN** which had not yet been converted to a **SHOFAR**. It was twisted, covered with thick ridges and bumps. It was an ugly long **RAM**'s **HORN,** which was a blend of colors - brown's, blacks, grays, and opaque colors. Right before my eyes, there appeared to the right of this **HORN** another **HORN**. I knew within my heart it was the same **HORN** that had gone through an incredible transformation.

This **HORN** was much straighter, polished, and beautiful. It glowed with the previous colors, but now they were beautiful compared to its former dull ugliness. I instantly knew in my heart that the old **HORN** had been useless in its unfinished condition. It was filled with nothing but cartridge. There is no way that the mystical winds of **God** could blow through it and bring forth a majestic **THUNDER**.

The finished **HORN** I saw within my mind's eye was completely hollowed out. The old nature, the old flesh, the old ways had been removed. There now ran a **Holy** air vent all the way through the **HORN** of this transformed **RAM's HORN**.

It was no longer just merely a dead, lifeless, useless **HORN**, but it had become a sacred instrument to be used in the **Divine** plans and purposes of **God**. It had become A **Holy SHOFAR**! I knew all of this instantly within my heart. I knew within my heart that this **SHOFAR** was symbolic of the complete yielded life of a believer!

The Amazing Significance of the SHOFAR (part 2)

Since 1975 I have had the privilege of teaching and preaching the gospel. The Lord has allowed me to minister over 10,000 sermons. I know some ministers that seem to struggle in their endeavor to put together a message. I can honestly say that very seldom do I ever have a lack of material.

Most of my messages come directly from the inspiration of **Divine Visitations**. Many times I have seen myself preaching a message in a dream. I cannot tell you the times that I had set-aside notes I had prepared because the Lord had given me a dream the night before. The word of **God**, revelations, truth is like rivers of water that keep flowing from the throne room of **God**.

When I had this open vision on Tuesday, the **Spirit** began to quicken to me on the importance of the **Spirit**ual significance of the **SHOFAR**! What almost always happens when I have one of these supernatural experiences is that a **Spirit**ual hunger rises within my heart to investigate what it is that the Lord is showing me.

Immediately I began to search and investigate the **SHOFAR**! **The Bible is filled with thousands of types, shadows, patterns, illustrations, and examples of who, what, how, why, where, and when.**

The SHOFAR is a powerful declaration of who and what the believers are to be in CHRIST

First, let us look at the importance of the **SHOFAR**. There are so many different realities that we could look at dealing with the **SHOFAR** that there simply is not enough time for me to share these critical truths with you. Where I believe in my heart that the Lord wants me to go in this teaching is in the preparation of the **RAM**'s **HORN** to be turned into a **SHOFAR** that can be used by **God**.

The first mentioning of the **SHOFAR** (**TRUMPET**) is found in the book of Exodus chapter 19.

Exodus 19:16 And it came to pass on the third day in the morning, that there were THUNDERs and lightnings, and a thick cloud upon the mount, and the VOICE of the TRUMPET exceeding loud; so that all the people that was in the camp trembled.........:19 And when

the VOICE of the TRUMPET sounded long, and waxed louder and louder, Moses spake, and God answered him by a VOICE. 20:18 And all the people saw the THUNDERINGs, and the lightnings, and the noise of the TRUMPET, and the mountain smoking: and when the people saw it, they removed, and stood afar off.

This **THUNDERING**, lightnings with the **VOICE** of the **TRUMPET** exceedingly loud is exceptionally significant. It is a type of the **VOICE** of **God**. This is also true when we become a pure and **Holy SHOFAR**. The **VOICE** of **God** will come **THUNDERING** forth by the **Spirit** of the Lord.

2 Samuel 22:14 The Lord THUNDERed from heaven, and the most High uttered his VOICE.

Job 37:4 After it a VOICE roareth: he THUNDEReth with the VOICE of his excellency; and he will not stay them when his VOICE is heard.

Job 37:5 God THUNDEReth marvelously with his VOICE; great things doeth he, which we cannot comprehend.

Job 40:9 Hast thou an arm like God? or canst thou THUNDER with a VOICE like him?

Psalm 18:13 The Lord also THUNDERed in the heavens, and the Highest gave his VOICE; hail stones and coals of FIRE.

Psalm 29:3 The VOICE of the Lord is upon the waters: the God of glory THUNDEReth: the Lord is upon many waters.

I WENT TO HEAVEN

In 1975 approximately two months after I had been saved, I had an amazing experience when an Angel of the Lord took me to heaven. In part of this experience, I stood upon the sea of glass before the Lord, who was Sitting upon His Throne. The **FATHER** began to speak to me. It was like streaks of lightning hitting my body, and exploding inside of me like the roaring of the **THUNDER**. This is **The TRUMPET of God**!

Before the Throne

I fell as one dead before the throne, quivering and shaking before the presence of **God**. Then a **VOICE** spoke forth as if coming from everywhere. It filled my mind and heart with shaking and trembling. This **VOICE** was filled with absolute complete and total authority and **Holiness**.

I knew it was the **FATHER**'s **VOICE** that was speaking to me. As I lay on my face before the throne of **God**, I heard unspeakable words that can not be uttered with human vocabulary. It was literally as if streaks of lightning were hitting my body with every word that He spoke. His words hit my body; they would explode in me like the soundings of **THUNDER.**

My whole body shook and vibrated uncontrollably at these **THUNDERING**s. These **THUNDERING**'s flooded my body, my soul, my mind, my emotions, and possessed me like as if I was hanging on to a high voltage line. It had to be **God** supernaturally strengthening me to keep me alive through this experience.

I am convinced that if you had been standing from a distance, you would have seen streaks of **Divine** lightning and **FIRE** coming out of **God**'s mouth and striking my body. This **Divine** lightning and **FIRE** were not meant to destroy me, but to some extent, was intended to impregnate me with **God**'s **Divine** purposes, plans, and abilities.

I knew that my inner man was drinking deeply of the mysteries and perfect plans of **God**. I remember the tears flowing from my eyes, down my face as I listened to the Word of the Lord. A pool of tears gathered upon the sea of glass as I wept before the Lord. The glory of **God** was all around, upon, and in me. My body was enveloped in a glistening cloud of energy. Through this whole experience, I laid there weeping and whispering "Thank you, **JESUS**, Thank you **FATHER**" over and over.

I did not understand with my mind what was transpiring, but I knew in my heart that **God** was speaking to me **Divine** truths and mysteries, that which was to be accomplished and would shortly happen. I knew that He was supernaturally impregnating me with the grace that was necessary to achieve His purposes in my life. This seemed to go on forever. Then as quickly as it had started, it was over. The **Spirit** of the Lord whisked me instantly away from the throne room of **God**.

The TRUMPET Is Symbolic of Gods VOICE

Heaven is filled with the sounding of the **TRUMPET**. It is a powerful declaration of the authority, power, and majesty of **God**. YouTube is full of mysterious sounds of **HORN**s that are blasting in the heavens throughout the world. Many have tried to explain these strange sounds but to no scientific evidence. Could these sounds be the call of **God** to humans to repent, and to fall to their faces, surrendering their lives to him?

Revelation 1:10 I was in the Spirit on the Lord's day and heard behind me a great VOICE, as of a TRUMPET,

Revelation 4:1 After this I looked, and, behold, a door was opened in heaven: and the first VOICE which I heard was as it were of a TRUMPET talking with me; which said, Come up hither, and I will shew thee things which must be hereafter.

Revelation 8:2 And I saw the seven angels which stood before God; and to them were given seven TRUMPETs.............:6 And the seven angels which had the seven TRUMPETs prepared themselves to sound.

I saw Seven Angels, with Seven TRUMPETs!

The coming tsunami (I had an open vision, 2008). I was up early one morning in deep prayer when my heart was quickened to look off to the east. Of course, I'm standing in my house, so all I can see is the east front room wall, with Windows, the curtains, and the plastered white ceiling. But at that very moment, something supernatural happened, the heavens were instantly opened to me.

I was completely amazed because as I was looking up, I saw Seven Angelic Beings Standing in the Heavens. They all had golden **TRUMPET**s (extended **RAM HORN**s) lifted to their lips. I perceived that they had not yet started to blow the seven **TRUMPET**s, but they were about to. Then I looked off to the left of these seven angelic beings, with the seven golden **RAM HORN**s in their hands lifted to their lips. And there before me was an army beyond count upon horses.

In front of this massive army of Saints dressed in white, there was a man in white on a white horse. There was a gleaming golden crown upon his head, and on his side, was written**: The Word of God**! Behind this army was the largest wave of water I had ever seen. It was coming up over the top of them: a massive wave, a tsunami of water. Immediately I knew within my heart that this was the early and latter rain coming together and that it was about to hit the Earth. And after this outpouring, the seven angels would begin to blow their **TRUMPET**s. Judgment would come to the earth.

I stood there in total shock and amazement looking at this open supernatural vision. Knowing that these angels with the seven golden **RAM HORN**s to their lips had already filled their lungs with air, and were only waiting for the **King of Kings and Lord of Lords** to permit them to blow these **TRUMPET**s. We are about to enter a fantastic time. I believe it is almost upon us.

The Amazing Significance of the SHOFAR (part 3)

There is an important truth revealed to us in the book of Zechariah. Let us look at this Scripture in contexts.

Zechariah 9: 14 And the Lord shall be seen over them, and his arrow shall go forth as the lightning: and the Lord God shall blow the TRUMPET, and shall go with whirlwinds of the south.

15 The Lord of hosts shall defend them, and they shall devour, and subdue with sling stones; and they shall drink, and make a noise as through wine; and they shall be filled like bowls, and as the corners of the altar.

16 And the Lord their God shall save them in that day as the flock of his people: for they shall be as the stones of a crown, lifted up as an ensign upon his land.

17 For how great is his goodness, and how great is his beauty! corn shall make the young men cheerful, and new wine the maids.

Notice in verse 14 that the Lord says He, Himself shall blow the **TRUMPET**. There is such a profound and **Divine** mystery in **God** blowing the **TRUMPET** that it is beyond human comprehension. The what, the when, the where, and the why of the **TRUMPET** of **God** is truly amazing. We will try to bring forth some of these truths in this book.

There is another Scripture that declares **God** using the **TRUMPET**.

Isaiah 18:3 All ye inhabitants of the world, and dwellers on the earth, see ye, when he lifteth up an ensign on the mountains; and when he bloweth a TRUMPET, hear ye.

Blow Ye the TRUMPET

Blowing the **TRUMPET (SHOFAR)** within the Scriptures, there has always been a revelation of the audible **VOICE** and will of the **FATHER**. The Israelites blew the **TRUMPET** for many reasons, on many occasions. Some of these reasons and circumstances we will share with you. What I would like to emphasize now is that at the sounding of the **TRUMPET** (which is the audible **VOICE** of **God** speaking) was not just for his people, but for all of humanity.

Within that **THUNDER**ous sound, there can be heard the very heart of **God**. Those who have ears that hear will hear **God**'s **VOICE** in the **THUNDERING** of the **TRUMPET**. When John the Baptist finished baptizing **JESUS**, it is said that the people heard a sound like that of **THUNDER**. But **JESUS** and John the Baptist heard the **FATHER** say this: this is my beloved son in whom I am well pleased.

Matthew 3:17 And lo a VOICE from heaven, saying, This is my beloved Son, in whom I am well pleased.

John 12:28 FATHER, glorify thy name. Then came there a VOICE from heaven, saying, I have both glorified it, and will glorify it again.29 The people therefore, that stood by, and heard it, said that it THUNDERed: others said, An angel spake to him.30 JESUS answered and said, This VOICE came not because of me, but for your sakes.

I believe that all the Scriptures, the prophetic words, the truths that the prophets of Old Testament and the apostles, prophets, pastors, evangelist, and teachers of the New Testament have spoken forth, was the wind of **God**'s **Spirit** manifested in their **VOICE**s. What a great mystery this is. **JESUS** said in John that they who are born of the **Spirit** are like the wind. From whence they come, and whence they go, no man knows. They are born of the water and the **Spirit**.

The wind blows through these majestic **TRUMPET**s (**SHOFAR**s) wrapped in human flesh. It is the **THUNDER**ous, booming, blasting **VOICE** Of the Eternal, Immortal, and Everlasting **God**. **JESUS** himself was the **VOICE** of the **FATHER** in human flesh, speaking to humanity. The **TRUMPET** can be blown very loud or very softly. This sound has no end to its multiple ranges. There's a man by the name of Phil Driscoll who can take the **SHOFAR** and play it like a professional **TRUMPET**. There are many types of wind instruments which depend upon the lung capacity, and the breath of the one who is playing the instrument.

Some of these instruments are **TRUMPET**s, trombones, euphoniums, flutes, cornet, tubas, and saxophones. These are some of the traditional wind instruments. The instruments must be blown into a mouthpiece to get their unique musical sound. All these devices contain a resonator, or tube, in which air is set to vibrate to produce the required pitch. The **SHOFAR (RAM**'s **HORN TRUMPET**) is one of the oldest wind instruments known to man.

The wind that is blowing through these instruments is an illustration of the **Spirit** of **God** moving through a **sanctified, dedicated, surrendered Believer**. **JESUS CHRIST** himself was completely surrendered to the **Spirit** and the will of his heavenly **FATHER**. There are many Scriptures to verify this biblical reality.

Luke 4:17 And there was delivered unto him the book of the prophet Esaias. And when he had opened the book, he found the place where it was written,18 The Spirit of the Lord is upon me, because he hath anointed me to preach the gospel to

the poor; he hath sent me to heal the brokenhearted, to preach deliverance to the captives, and recovering of sight to the blind, to set at liberty them that are bruised,19 To preach the acceptable year of the Lord.

John 6:63 It is the Spirit that quickeneth; the flesh profiteth nothing: the words that I speak unto you, they are Spirit, and they are life.

John 12:49 For I have not spoken of myself; but the FATHER which sent me, he gave me a commandment, what I should say, and what I should speak.50 And I know that his commandment is life everlasting: whatsoever I speak therefore, even as the FATHER said unto me, so I speak.

2 Thessalonians 2:8 And then shall that Wicked be revealed, whom the Lord shall consume with the Spirit of his mouth, and shall destroy with the brightness of his coming:

Even as the wind of the **Spirit** spoke through **CHRIST**, so the wind of the **Spirit** is meant to speak through the **VOICE** of **God**'s people. We are to lift our **VOICE** like a **TRUMPET** to declare the everlasting gospel to the four corners of the earth, and every creature. As we are **surrendered and submitted** to the will of the **FATHER**, it will not be you speaking, but Him speaking through us. On the day of Pentecost, when the **Holy** Ghost fell upon the disciples of **JESUS**, there came like a sound of a mighty rushing wind.

Acts 2:1 And when the day of Pentecost was fully come, they

were all with one accord in one place.2 And suddenly there came a sound from heaven as of a rushing mighty wind, and it filled all the house where they were sitting. 3 And there appeared unto them cloven tongues like as of FIRE, and it sat upon each of them.

2 Peter 1:20 Knowing this first, that no prophecy of the scripture is of any private interpretation.21 For the prophecy came not in old time by the will of man: but Holy men of God spake as they were moved by the Holy Ghost.

We were created to be instruments of **God**'s righteousness. Musical instruments in **God**'s wonderful orchestra. It is not the breath of a natural man that brings forth this mystical sound of the gospel. It is the very **Spirit** of the living **God**. It is the melodious **VOICE** of our beautiful and blessed Savior. The sound that is coming forth is not flesh or confusion, but the **Divine** revelation of heaven.

Romans 6:13 Neither yield ye your members as instruments of unrighteousness unto sin: but yield yourselves unto God, as those that are alive from the dead, and your members as instruments of righteousness unto God.

THE MUSIC OF HEAVEN

This is an important **Visitation** that I would like to share with you. This amazing dream that I had is very difficult to describe in human words. I was sleeping peacefully when, at about three o'clock in the morning, I was suddenly smack dab in the middle of heaven, close to the throne of **God**. It was so real and tangible; it felt as if I was in heaven physically. At that moment, **God** gave me eyes to see all of existence. It was as if I was omnipresent. All of the creation lay before me. My mind and emotions and all five of my senses perceived all things. I embraced everything at one time.

It was the most amazing experience you could imagine. It was so beautiful and magnificent that it is beyond a precise description. It could be likened to being in the eye of a storm with everything spinning around you.

With this supernatural, imparted ability, I could perceive the **Spirit**ual and angelic. I saw angels of all types and ranks. I saw and felt the nature and physical realms. I saw the planets, moons, stars, solar systems, and the whole universe.

I saw animal life, plant life, oceans, seas, lakes, and rivers. I even saw the microscopic molecular realm. **God** supernaturally expanded my capacity mentally and emotionally to perceive all things. If it had not happened to me personally, I would be skeptical myself of someone saying these things.

During this experience, I began to be overtaken by an absolute sense of incredible harmony. **It was unity and oneness of an overwhelming proportion.** It resonated through my whole being. I could feel it in my bones, flesh, emotions, and mind. My heart resonated with His harmony.

My whole being was engulfed in this unbelievable symphony. All creation, the universe, and **Spirit**ual realm were in complete and total harmony and unity. Instantly I perceived everything was at one with **God**. Not one molecule, not one atom or proton was uncoordinated with **God**. As I was looking at creation, suddenly I perceived an invisible force permeating and saturating all of it.

God gave me eyes to see this invisible force. I could see it moving, flowing, and penetrating everything. With this ability to see, He also gave me **Spirit**ual understanding. I realized at that moment that it was this incredible invisible force which was causing all things to exist and flow and move as one living, breathing creation.

What I am sharing with you was a progressive revelation unfolding before me like a flower blossoming. During this experience, my ears opened, and I heard the most incredible music, a breathtaking song. This invisible force was a song that was being sung. Instantly I perceived that it was this music, this song, which was holding all of creation together. This song was permeating every animate and inanimate thing together.

Not only was it holding everything together but also everything was singing along with it. It was the most incredible music and song you could ever imagine. It is beyond comprehension or human ability to describe this song and what it was doing. All of creation was being upheld and kept together by this song. I could see it and feel it. **It was inside of me**. I was a part of it. No maestro, psalmist, no Beethoven, or Mozart could ever produce such a majestic and grand **Master**piece.

As I watched and listened, I was overwhelmed with the reality that it was this song that was causing everything to be in harmony and unity. It was this song causing everything to live, move, exist, and have its being.

During this experience, curiosity took hold of me. I began to wonder, where is this music, this song, coming from? I began to look high and low, trying to discover where this song had originated. I finally looked behind me, and on a higher elevation, I saw **God** sitting upon His throne.

I did not see the clarity of **God**'s form or face. He was covered in a glistening mist, somewhat like fog. But as I looked upon His form, it was as if my eyes zoomed in on His mouth. I was looking intently at the mouth of **God**. Out of His mouth was coming this amazing, beautiful, awesome song.

This song that **God** was singing was holding everything together and in perfect harmony. **God** the **FATHER** was making everything one with Himself through this song, this music coming out of His mouth. I literally could see, feel, and experience the song coming out of **God**'s mouth. In my heart, I said to the **FATHER**, "**FATHER**, how long will You sing this song?" And He spoke to me in my heart, "Throughout eternity; MY **VOICE** will never cease to sing.

My **VOICE** will never cease to be heard." I could see letters streaming from **God**'s mouth. Words were coming forth from His mouth. They were swimming in a river of transparent life, like fish swimming in a river. These words seemed to be alive. They were spreading throughout the entire universe, causing everything to exist and to be in harmony. They were permeating all of creation, visible and invisible, **Spirit**ual, and natural.

I knew in my heart that this was the Word of **God**, the **Divine**ly inspired Scriptures. The Word was swimming as if in an invisible, transparent river. I knew that this river was a living, quickening force. I knew that it was this river which was causing the Word of **God** to be alive. The Word of **God** was being carried forth by this river. I said to the **FATHER**, "**FATHER**, what is this river that the Word is flowing, swimming, and living in?" And He said to my heart, "It is the **Holy** Ghost!"

I was stunned into silence. After a while, I repeated my question. Once again, He said to me, "It is the **Holy** Ghost. It is the breath of My mouth coming from the **VOICE** of My lips. And this **VOICE** is My Son, **JESUS CHRIST**.

My VOICE is My Son, JESUS CHRIST

And out of His **VOICE** comes the **Holy** Ghost and My Word." Further, He said to me, "My Word would not sustain, heal, deliver, or bring life unless it is quickened and made alive by My **Spirit**."

Then the **FATHER** confirmed this to me by quoting the Scripture where **JESUS** said, "My Words are **Spirit**, and they are life." (See John 6:63.) The **FATHER** spoke to me again and said, "You can quote, memorize, and declare the whole Bible, but it will be dead and lifeless until you yield, surrender, move, flow, and come into complete harmony with the Word of **God** and the **Holy** Ghost."

This I believe, to some extent, reveals **God**'s eternal purpose for you and me: to be in complete oneness and harmony with **God**, the **FATHER**, the Son, and the **Holy** Ghost!

The Amazing Significance of the SHOFAR (part 4)

Man, Is a Complex Intricate Musical Instrument

Psalm 100 Make a joyful noise unto the Lord, all ye lands. Serve the Lord with gladness: come before his presence with singing. Know ye that the Lord he is God: it is he that hath made us, and not we ourselves; we are his people, and the sheep of his pasture.

Even as the of blowing air through a **TRUMPET** or a musical wind instrument produces sound, music, melodies, and harmonies, so man himself is a fabulous walking, talking, thinking, and living musical instrument that **God** has created.

Psalm 139:14 I will praise thee; for I am fearfully and wonderfully made: marvelous are thy works; and that my soul knoweth right well.

The human **VOICE** consists of sound that is made by a person blowing air from his lungs and using the vocal folds for talking, singing, laughing, crying, screaming, etc. The human **VOICE** frequency is specifically a part of human sound production in which the vocal folds (vocal cords) are the primary sound source.

Generally speaking, the mechanism for generating the human **VOICE** can be subdivided into three parts; the **lungs**, the **vocal folds** within the **larynx**, and the **articulators.** The lung (the pump) must produce adequate airflow and air pressure to **vibrate vocal folds**. This **air pressure** is the fuel of the **VOICE**.

*** It is the Spirit of God that gives VOICE to the will of God, being declared prophetically to the mouth of a believer.**

The vocal folds (vocal cords) are a vibrating valve that chops up the airflow from the lungs into audible pulses that form the laryngeal sound source. The muscles of the larynx adjust the length and tension of the vocal folds to 'fine-**Tune**' pitch and tone.

The articulators **(the parts of the vocal tract above the larynx consisting of tongue, palate, cheek, lips, etc.)** articulate and filter the sound emanating from the larynx and to some degree can interact with the laryngeal airflow to strengthen it or weaken it as a sound source.

The vocal folds, in combination with the articulators, can produce highly intricate arrays of sound. The tone of **VOICE** may be modulated to suggest emotions such as anger, surprise, or happiness. Singers use the human **VOICE** as an instrument for creating music.

The sound of everyone's **VOICE** is unique not only because of the actual shape and size of an individual's vocal cords but also due to the size and shape of the rest of that person's body, especially the vocal tract, and the manner in which the speech sounds are habitually formed and articulated. Humans have vocal folds that can loosen, tighten, or change their thickness, over which breath can be transferred at varying pressures.

The shape of the chest and neck, the position of the tongue, and the tightness of otherwise unrelated muscles can be altered. Anyone of these actions results in a change in pitch, volume, timbre, or tone of the sound produced. Sound also resonates within different parts of the body, and an individual's size and bone structure can affect somewhat the sound generated by an individual.

Singers can also learn to project sound in certain ways so that it resonates better within their vocal tract. This is known as vocal resonation. Another significant influence on vocal sound and production is the function of the larynx, which people can manipulate in different ways to produce different sounds. These various kinds of laryngeal function are described as different kinds of vocal registers.

(https://en.wikipedia.org/wiki/Human_VOICE)

With our vocal cords, we can sing and speak many different styles of music, languages, and words! There are roughly 6,500 spoken languages in the world today. However, about 2,000 of these languages have fewer than 1,000 speakers. The most popular language in the world is Mandarin Chinese and has approximately 1,213,000,000 people in the world that speak this particular language.

One of the most misunderstood, and least spoken languages of the world is the **language of heaven**! The language of heaven when it is spoken out of the mouth of a believer by the **Spirit** of Faith and **The Quickening Spirit Of God** produces life = **ZOE** (life as **God** has it). What a beautiful and profound song is produced when we have become **Gods Sanctified TRUMPETs**, by which the wind of the **Spirit** brings forth **incredible Power, Authority, and Life.**

MUSIC

There are so many different styles of music that there is not room enough to share them all with you. There is believed to be over 93 million songs that have been written and sung by men. If you were to pull back the curtains of heaven, we would see that heaven is filled with singing, music, and **Divine** instruments of worship.

Psalm 144:9 I will sing a new song unto thee, O God: upon a psaltery and an instrument of ten strings will I sing praises unto thee.

Revelation 5:9 And they sung a new song, saying, Thou art worthy to take the book, and to open the seals thereof: for thou wast slain, and hast redeemed us to God by thy blood out of every kindred, and tongue, and people, and nation;

GOD, HIMSELF SINGS

The Scriptures declare that **God** himself sings over his people.

Zephaniah 3:17 The Lord thy God in the midst of thee is mighty; he will save, he will rejoice over thee with joy; he will rest in his love, he will joy over thee with singing.

We are told that the Lord **JESUS CHRIST** sang right before he went to Gethsemane and then to Golgotha. This was on the first Thursday, right after the Last Supper which is on the first day of Passover. Mark and Matthew record this event,

"And when they had sung a hymn they went out to the Mount of Olives" (Matthew 26:30, Mark 14:26).

* In The Complete Jewish Bible (CJB, Jewish New Testament Publications) Matthew 26:30 reads, **"After singing the Hallel"** For centuries before that first Maundy Thursday, the Jewish people always sang the **Hallel** at the meal at the end of the first day of Passover. Observant Jews still do.

Unless **JESUS** and His eleven Jewish disciples ignored the tradition of centuries, they sang **Psalms 113-118** (or selected stanzas from them) that night. They probably sang one part before the meal and another part after the meal.

Almost certainly, the one song we know **JESUS** did sing is **Psalms 113-118**. What do you imagine **JESUS** felt as He sang these words?

The stone the builders rejected has become the cornerstone; the Lord has done this, and it is marvelous in our eyes (Psalm 118: 22-23).

With the torturous crucifixion, just hours ahead, what did **JESUS** think as the **12-VOICE** ensemble sang these lines?

Precious in the sight of the Lord is the death of his faithful servants (Psalm 116:15).

With Judas gone out into the night, and with the meal ended, and the eleven standing around the empty platter, **JESUS** sang,

With the Lord on my side, I do not fear. What can mortals do to me? The Lord is on my side to help me (Psalm 118:6-7).

I believe that Easter was brimming in our Lord's heart as He sang,

I will not die but live, and will proclaim what the Lord has done (Psalm 118:17 KJV).

(Written by Wesley D. Tracy who teaches Christian preaching and adult education at Nazarene Theological Seminary.)

..

CHAPTER TWO

The What, When, Where and Why of the Blowing of the TRUMPET!

Blowing the SHOFAR is an inseparable part of the atmosphere of The Days of Awe and The High Holidays.

The Ram's HORN

The **SHOFAR** is usually made from a ram's **HORN**. A ram is a male sheep at least one-year-old. Exceptionally long and twisted **SHOFARs**, like the ones popular among Yemenite Jews, are made from bushbuck **HORNs**. The bushbuck is a type of antelope, living in the edges of the African deserts.

Some say that the word **SHOFAR** is derived from two Hebrew words – Shor + Par (bull and ox); but a bull's **HORN** can not serve as a **SHOFAR** because it would remind us of the sin of the golden calf.

We do not have in Israel rams or antelopes with **HORN**s adequate for **SHOFAR** making. The **HORN**s are brought from various places around the world, mostly from Morocco, Algeria, and countries in southern Africa. (From the Internet)

This particular portion could be filled with a massive amount of information, but that is not the purpose of this book. Where I need to take, you are to the transformation of a dead **RAM**'s **HORN**, into the beautiful instrument of a polished, glorious, sanctified, **THUNDERING SHOFAR**! It is necessary for us to have some enlightenment on the importance and the use of this **SHOFAR**!

Understand that the **TRUMPET** was of extreme importance in Jewish culture, customs, and history. There are many instances of it being used in the old and the New Testament. When you search the word **TRUMPET** and **HORN,** all told together; it is mentioned approximately 200 times.

TRUMPET - All (104) Old Testament (92) New Testament (12)

HORN -All (93) Old Testament (83) New Testament (10)

Here a list of 21 of the reasons, circumstance, and time that I could find for the **TRUMPET** when it was used.

#1 For the Sabbath

*** Leviticus 23:24 Speak unto the children of Israel, saying, In the seventh month, in the first day of the month, shall ye have a sabbath, a memorial of blowing of TRUMPETs, an Holy Convocation.**

***Numbers 29:1 And in the seventh month, on the first day of the month, ye shall have an Holy convocation; ye shall do no servile work: it is a day of blowing the TRUMPETs unto you.**

***Psalm 81:3Blow up the TRUMPET in the new moon, in the time appointed, on our solemn feast day.**

#2 To WARN the People

***Numbers 10:(3-10) 6 When ye blow an alarm the second time, then the camps that lie on the south side shall take their journey: they shall blow an alarm for their journeys.**

***Ezekiel 33:3 If when he seeth the sword come upon the land, he blow the TRUMPET, and warn the people;:4 Then whosoever heareth the sound of the TRUMPET, and taketh not warning; if the sword come, and take him away, his blood shall be upon his own head.:5 He heard the sound of the TRUMPET, and took not warning; his blood shall be upon him. But he that taketh warning shall deliver his soul.6 But if the watchman see the sword come, and blow not the TRUMPET, and the people be not warned; if the sword come, and take any person from among them, he is taken away in his iniquity; but his blood will I require at the watchman's hand.**

***Jeremiah 6:17 Also I set watchmen over you, saying, Hearken to the sound of the TRUMPET. But they said, We will not hearken.**

#3 Blow the TRUMPET for Gathering

***Numbers 10:7 But when the congregation is to be gathered together, ye shall blow, but ye shall not sound an alarm.8 And the sons of Aaron, the priests, shall blow with the TRUMPETs; and they shall be to you for an ordinance for ever throughout your generations.8 And the sons of Aaron, the priests, shall blow with the TRUMPETs; and they shall be to you for an ordinance for ever throughout your generations.**

***Judges 6:34 But the Spirit of the Lord came upon Gideon, and he blew a TRUMPET; and Abiezer was gathered after him.**

#4 To Declare WAR

***Numbers 31:6 And Moses sent them to the war, a thousand of every tribe, them and Phinehas the son of Eleazar the priest, to the war, with the Holy instruments, and the TRUMPETs to blow in his hand.**

#5 To Get Gods Attention

***Numbers 10:9 And if ye go to war in your land against the enemy that oppresseth you, then ye shall blow an alarm with the TRUMPETs; and ye shall be remembered before the Lord your God, and ye shall be saved from your enemies.**

#6 On days of Gladness, Solemn Days, New Month, Over Sacrifices.

***Numbers 10:10 Also in the day of your gladness, and in your solemn days, and in the beginnings of your months, ye shall blow with the TRUMPETs over your burnt offerings, and over the sacrifices of your peace offerings; that they may be to you for a memorial before your God: I am the Lord your God.**

***2 Chronicles 29:27 And Hezekiah commanded to offer the burnt offering upon the altar. And when the burnt offering began, the song of the Lord began also with the TRUMPETs, and with the instruments ordained by David king of Israel.**

#7 The Day of the Lord

***Joel 2:1 Blow ye the TRUMPET in Zion, and sound an alarm in my Holy mountain: let all the inhabitants of the land tremble: for the day of the Lord cometh, for it is nigh at hand;**

***Jeremiah 51:27 Set ye up a standard in the land, blow the TRUMPET among the nations, prepare the nations against her, call together against her the kingdoms of Ararat, Minni, and Ashchenaz; appoint a captain against her; cause the horses to come up as the rough caterpillers.**

#8 To Bring Down the Walls of Your Enemies

***Joshua 6:4 And seven priests shall bear before the ark seven TRUMPETs of RAMS' HORNs: and the seventh day ye shall compass the city seven times, and the priests shall blow with the TRUMPETs.:5 And it shall come to pass, that when they make a long blast with the RAM's HORN, and when ye hear the sound of the TRUMPET, all the people shall shout with a great shout; and the wall of the city shall fall down flat, and the people shall ascend up every man straight before him.**

***Joshua 6:13 And seven priests bearing seven TRUMPETs of RAMS' HORNs before the ark of the Lord went on continually, and blew with the TRUMPETs: and the armed men went before them; but the rereward came after the ark of the Lord, the priests going on, and blowing with the TRUMPETs.**

***Joshua 6:20 So the people shouted when the priests blew with the TRUMPETs: and it came to pass, when the people heard the sound of the TRUMPET, and the people shouted with a great shout, that the wall fell down flat, so that the people went up into the city, every man straight before him, and they took the city.**

#9 To Bring Repentance

***Isaiah 58:1 Cry aloud, spare not, lift up thy VOICE like a TRUMPET, and shew my people their transgression, and the house of Jacob their sins.**

***2 Chronicles 13:11 And they burn unto the Lord every morning and every evening burnt sacrifices and sweet incense: the shewbread also set they in order upon the pure table; and the candlestick of gold with the lamps thereof, to burn every evening: for we keep the charge of the Lord our God; but ye have forsaken him.12 And, behold, God himself is with us for our captain, and his priests with sounding TRUMPETs to cry alarm against you. O children of Israel, fight ye not against the Lord God of your FATHERs; for ye shall not prosper.**

***2 Chronicles 13:12 And, behold, God himself is with us for our captain, and his priests with sounding TRUMPETs to cry alarm against you. O children of Israel, fight ye not against the Lord God of your FATHERs; for ye shall not prosper.**

***Jeremiah 4:19 My bowels, my bowels! I am pained at my very heart; my heart maketh a noise in me; I cannot hold my peace, because thou hast heard, O my soul, the sound of the TRUMPET, the alarm of war.**

***Joel 2:15 Blow the TRUMPET in Zion, sanctify a fast, call a solemn assembly:**

#10 Commitment to the LORD

***2 Chronicles 15:14 And they sware unto the Lord with a loud VOICE, and with shouting, and with TRUMPETs, and with cornets.**

#11 To Get Victory Over the Enemy

***Judges 7:18 When I blow with a TRUMPET, I and all that are with me, then blow ye the TRUMPETs also on every side of all the camp, and say, The sword of the Lord, and of Gideon.**

***Judges 7:20 And the three companies blew the TRUMPETs,**

and brake the pitchers, and held the lamps in their left hands, and the TRUMPETs in their right hands to blow withal: and they cried, The sword of the Lord, and of Gideon.

***Judges 7:22 And the three hundred blew the TRUMPETs, and the Lord set every man's sword against his fellow, even throughout all the host: and the host fled to Bethshittah in Zererath, and to the border of Abelmeholah, unto Tabbath.**

#12 For Safety and Protection

***Nehemiah 4:18 For the builders, everyone had his sword girded by his side, and so builded. And he that sounded the TRUMPET was by me.**

***Nehemiah 4:20 In what place therefore ye hear the sound of the TRUMPET, resort ye thither unto us: our God shall fight for us.**

#13 Anointing of a New King

***1 Kings 1:34 And let Zadok the priest and Nathan the**

prophet anoint him there king over Israel: and blow ye with the TRUMPET, and say, God save king Solomon.

***1 Kings 1:39 And Zadok the priest took an HORN of oil out of the tabernacle, and anointed Solomon. And they blew the TRUMPET; and all the people said, God save king Solomon.**

#14 It Signifies the Presence of God

***Exodus 20:18 And all the people saw the THUNDERINGs, and the lightnings, and the noise of the TRUMPET, and the mountain smoking: and when the people saw it, they removed, and stood afar off.**

***Psalm 47:5 God is gone up with a shout, the Lord with the sound of a TRUMPET.**

***2 Chronicles 5:13 It came even to pass, as the TRUMPETers and singers were as one, to make one sound to be heard in praising and thanking the Lord; and when they lifted up their VOICE with the TRUMPETs and cymbals and instruments of musick, and praised the Lord, saying, For he is good; for his mercy endureth for ever: that then the house was filled with a cloud, even the house of the Lord;**

#15 To WORSHIP The LORD

***Psalm 98:6 With TRUMPETs and sound of cornet make a joyful noise before the Lord, the King.**

***Psalm 150:3 Praise him with the sound of the TRUMPET: praise him with the psaltery and harp.**

***1 Chronicles 13:8 And David and all Israel played before God with all their might, and with singing, and with harps, and with psalteries, and with timbrels, and with cymbals, and with TRUMPETs.**

***1 Chronicles 15:28 Thus all Israel brought up the ark of the covenant of the Lord with shouting, and with sound of the cornet, and with TRUMPETs, and with cymbals, making a noise with psalteries and harps.**

***2 Chronicles 29:28 And all the congregation worshipped, and the singers sang, and the TRUMPETers sounded: and all this continued until the burnt offering was finished.**

#16 Signifies FREEDOM

***Leviticus 25:9 Then shalt thou cause the TRUMPET of the jubile to sound on the tenth day of the seventh month, in the day of atonement shall ye make the TRUMPET sound throughout all your land.**

#17 To Prepare the Way of the LORD

***2 Samuel 6:15 So David and all the house of Israel brought up the ark of the Lord with shouting, and with the sound of the TRUMPET.**

#18 Priest Were the Designated Users

***Nehemiah 4:20 In what place therefore ye hear the sound of the TRUMPET, resort ye thither unto us: our God shall fight for us.**

***Ephesians 4:11 And he gave some, apostles; and some, prophets; and some, evangelists; and some, pastors and teachers;**

#19 For the PREACHING of the WORD

***Hebrews 12:19 And the sound of a TRUMPET, and the VOICE of words; which VOICE they that heard intreated that the word should not be spoken to them any more:**

#20 THE GATHERING OF THE SAINTS

***Matthew 24:31 And he shall send his angels with a great sound of a TRUMPET, and they shall gather together his elect from the four winds, from one end of heaven to the other.**

***1 Corinthians 15:52 In a moment, in the twinkling of an eye, at the last trump: for the TRUMPET shall sound, and the dead shall be raised incorruptible, and we shall be changed.**

#21 COMING JUDGEMENT

***Hosea 8:1 Set the TRUMPET to thy mouth. He shall come as an eagle against the house of the Lord, because they have transgressed my covenant, and trespassed against my law.**

***Revelation 8:2 And I saw the seven angels which stood before God; and to them were given seven TRUMPETs.**

***Revelation 8:13 And I beheld, and heard an angel flying through the midst of heaven, saying with a loud VOICE, Woe, woe, woe, to the inhabiters of the earth by reason of the other VOICEs of the TRUMPET of the three angels, which are yet to sound!**

ALL ACCOMPLISHED BY ONE INSTRUMENT!

What does the TRUMPET represent?

It is the word of **God** being preached, proclaimed, and declared by the inspiration of the **Holy** Ghost. Within the WORD of **God** is revealed the will of **God**, the power of **God**, the nature of **God**, the life of **God**, the authority of **God**. There are many Scriptures that revealed this profound secret. When we preach this book underneath the tangible manifestation, impartation, empowerment of the **Spirit**, all Things Become Possible! Here are some of my own experiences when the Wind of the **Spirit** was moving through me.

THEY FELL to the Floor WEEPING!

(1981)

I was ministering in a German-speaking church called The Industrial Center of Germany. This church was situated about five stories up in a high-rise office complex. They did not have a pastor in this church at the time. They had a board of elders, and I understood one of the men was an oil tycoon. He was the one who supported all the activities and outreaches of the church.

I had an interpreter with us, who was a famous German worship leader and singer. When I preached at the church, I ministered a radical message on being one hundred percent, completely and sold out to **JESUS CHRIST**. I shared that there was a price to be paid to enter the deeper things of **God** and that you had to die to the flesh to live in the **Spirit**. **JESUS** gave His everything, and now it was our turn to give everything. About two-thirds of the way through this message, something amazing happened.

As I stood before the congregation to speak, the **Holy** Ghost began to move upon me in a mighty way dealing with the subject of being completely sold out 100% to **JESUS CHRIST**. The presence of **God** was manifested in a very strong and real way. Something amazing happened as I was about 35 to 45 minutes into my message.

All of a sudden, the **Spirit of God fell** upon that congregation in such a mighty way that everyone in that church **fell out of their chairs at once**. Instantly everyone in the congregation was on the floor weeping and wailing under the influence of the **Holy Spirit**. This was such a strange occurrence because neither my interpreter or I seem to be feeling or experiencing what everybody else was.

This happened in such a synchronized way that the thought came to me that for some reason, they had organized this as a church.

Because I no longer had their attention, I simply quit preaching, and got down on my knees, and started praying along with them. This continued for quite a while. Eventually, the weeping and crying stopped, and people began to get up and trickle away from the meeting. **No one was talking.** There was a **Holy** hush upon the whole congregation.

One of the leaders of the church invited us with a whisper down to the next floor, where there had been a meal prepared for us in the fellowship hall. As we sat down to eat, I could tell that they were all looking at me in a strange way. As my wife and I ate the food that was prepared to for us, nobody in the room spoke at all. I finally worked up enough courage to speak to the brother who was on my left. I simply asked the man if this happened very often?

He replied, **"Does what happen very often?"**

I said, **"Where all the people suddenly as one fall on the floor and start praying, crying and weeping?**

" He looked at me as if something was wrong. **He told me they had never seen or experienced anything like this before in their church services".**

This had been a **Divine** move of the **Holy** Ghost that came about as I was preaching on being completely sold out to **JESUS CHRIST.** The end results of this meeting was that the leadership of this church was so moved that they offered my wife and me to become their pastors. They told us that our financial needs were no concern because one of the brothers in the church was an oil tycoon.

I told them that I could not speak German, and therefore, I would not make a good pastor. They said this would be no problem because they would provide an interpreter unto I became fluent in their language. I got quiet before the Lord and asked him whether I should accept this offer? The Lord strongly spoke to my heart and said: No, I have other plans for you, and it is not my will for you to pastor this church. I informed them that I could not accept their offer, but that I was truly grateful and humbled by their request.

Atheist Saved, Healed, Delivered!

(2010)

Vicki, a dear sister in **CHRIST**, had come to me (being her pastor) with great concern about her sister Connie. Her sister was not only an atheist, but she had begun to dabble into satanic activities and was also experiencing great physical afflictions. On numerous occasions, Vicki came to the front of the church after service, and I prayed with her about her sister.

After one service, I perceived in my heart that if **God** did not **Divine**ly intervene in her sister's life in the very near future that not only would Connie lose her soul, but that she was headed for a very tragic death. I encouraged Vicki to go even deeper in prayer for her sister, and that I would join my prayers with hers. Up to this time, I had never met Connie, but the Lord had laid her upon my heart in a very real way.

The next time on Sunday, when I saw Vicki, I encouraged her to get her sister to come to one of our services. That I believed if **God** could get her sister to come up from West Virginia, he would do something amazing for her. Vicki began to encourage her sister strongly to attend one of our services, and yet she strongly resisted all of Vicki's encouragements.

One Sunday, Vicki came to me, informing me that her sister Connie had to be hospitalized for surgery. While she was in the hospital for surgery, she contracted a very deadly infection called MRSA. MRSA stands for methicillin-resistant Staphylococcus aureus. It is a "staph" germ that does not get better with many of antibiotics that usually cure staph infections. Most staph germs are spread by skin-to-skin contact (touching). A doctor, nurse, other health care provider, or visitors to a hospital may have staph germs on their body that can spread to a patient.

Once the staph germ enters the body, it can spread to bones, joints, the blood, or any organ, such as the lungs, heart, or brain. Serious staph infections are more common in people with chronic (long-term) medical problems. Each year, 90,000 Americans suffer from invasive MRSA infection, and about 20,000 dies.

The MRSA was so bad that the doctors had to put a stint in her chest where they could administer antibiotics a couple of times a day directly into her main arteries. When she finally was released from the hospital, a doctor from the CDC would go to her house several times a week. During all of this terrible situation, the **Spirit** of the Lord was able to move finally upon Connie's heart. She told her sister Vicki that she was going to come to one of our services no matter how difficult it was to have pastor mike pray for her.

Connie drove up from West Virginia to her sister Vicki's house one Sunday morning. That wonderful Sunday morning Vicki, Connie, and her sister Linda, all walked in together as that the service had already begun. **God** did an amazing miracle in Connie's life that morning. Vicki said: as we walked into the church, **GODS presence was so strong as you were Preaching that Linda and I started weeping right away**. We all three sat down as everyone in the congregation seemed to be also weeping in the service because of the presence of **God**.

During the service, my sister Connie had her eyes closed as she was praying and sincerely crying out to the Lord. During this time, the atheism that Connie had clung to, simply seem to melt off of her as if it had never existed. Connie later informed Linda and me that as she had her eyes closed, praying that she had heard a **VOICE** say: **Get on Your Knees!** She said within her heart she said that she could not do this because both of her kneecaps had been replaced with metal. She said the **VOICE** said to her again: **Get on Your Knees.**

This **VOICE** was so strong within her heart that she decided to do what she had heard, no matter what it took. At that very moment, Connie bent her legs and got down on her knees. As she went to her knees, Connie said that someone laid hands on her and was praying for her, she thought it was Pastor Mike at the time. Vicki, later on, said that she had seen her sister go to her knees, but that no one was there praying for her.

We now believe that it was **JESUS** himself laying his hands upon her sick, fevered, germ infested and broken body. At that very moment, **JESUS** completely healed Connie from the MRCA. Not only did the Lord deliver her from the staph infection, but healed her knees to where when she walked out of the church, she threw away her cane. That morning Connie gave her heart to **JESUS** and was filled with the **Holy** Ghost.

When Connie later went back to the hospital for bloodwork because of the MRCA, they kept testing her because they could not find the infection. Nine times they tested her for the MRCA but praised the Lord it was gone. This discovery completely shocked the doctors!

And these signs shall follow them that believe; In my name shall they cast out devils; they shall speak with new tongues; They shall take up serpents; and if they drink any deadly thing, it shall not hurt them; they shall lay hands on the sick, and they shall recover (Mark 16:17-18)

There Is Power In the Name of JESUS

(1980)

The **Spirit** of the Lord woke me up early one morning with a tremendous unction to pray. I went out into our little front room and began to pray in English and the **Spirit**. Before I knew it, I was lost in the **Holy** Ghost. When I finally quit praying, it seemed as if I had prayed for a very brief time. I looked at my watch and to my amazement, **seven to eight hours** had come and gone. During that whole time my wife never bothered me, she is wonderful in that way. When I am trying to press my way into the things of the **Spirit**, she simply leaves me alone.

The next morning the Lord woke me early again in prayer. I travailed and interceded in the **Spirit** and English. I was praying like a house on **FIRE** with deep groanings and urgencies in the **Holy** Ghost. When this burden partly lifted, it seemed as if I had prayed for only one or two hours. When I looked at my watch, another eight hours had come and gone! This continued for **seven or eight days, where the Spirit of God rolled me out of bed with a deep unction to pray! Every time that I prayed, it would only seem like an hour, and yet it was seven to eight hours had come and gone!** (I did not write down every day that this happened because I wasn't expecting it to happen.)

Right after this time of **Spirit-motivated intercession,** we had a wonderful move of **God**. The local ministerial that I was a part of was conducting a week-long community revival in the little town's pavilion. They wanted ministers to volunteer to speak. I agreed to do one of the services.

My wife, Kathleen, would lead the worship for this service, and I would preach the message. A lot of the local community came to these meetings. I was there every night to support the other pastors. I think our night was the last service. Kathleen and I had both had been praying and fasting, believing for **God** to do a mighty work. The host of the meeting opened with prayer and gave some announcements.

He introduced my wife and me as the pastors of the Three Springs Assembly of **God**. My wife did a wonderful job in leading worship. Then it was my turn. As I stood up to the pulpit, I sensed a great unction of the **Holy** Ghost to preach. I remember what I preached about The Name of **JESUS**. I'm not exaggerating when I tell you what happened. **The Spirit of God arrested everybody in that meeting**. It was like they were glued to their chairs. Their mouths were hanging open. The pastors looked like they were in shock. Then I gave an opportunity for people to be prayed for — the front of the pavilion filled with people wanting prayer.

After the service, the ministers came to me almost timidly. I was the youngest pastor among them. I was twenty-six years old now. Some of the older ministers seemed to be almost distraught. One of them said to me, **"No one ever taught me to preach like that!"** I told him it was the **Holy Ghost**. After that service, people from the community began to flock to our church. People were getting filled with the **Holy** Ghost everywhere.

And with many other words did he testify and exhort, saying, Save yourselves from this untoward generation. Then they that gladly received his word were baptized: and the same day there were added unto them about three thousand souls (Acts 2:40-41).

Like a Mighty Wind!

(1999)

One Sunday, as I was preaching, the **Holy** Ghost began to pour through me in a mighty way. The **Spirit** of the Lord was present in a powerful way to bring conviction to his people. Those presents began to be overwhelmed with a conviction of their sins. As I was preaching the power of **God** came through the midst of the congregation like a mighty whirlwind. People were being picked up out of their chairs and tossed around as if a miniature tornado was coming through the sanctuary.

After this experience, I had one of the sisters come to me saying that she felt herself being picked up and tossed across the room. I remember watching her flying through the air. Not one person that was tossed around had any injury or bruises. Some might doubt if this was of **God**, but it's because they are strangers to who **God** is. I have seen this same phenomenon on numerous occasions through the years as I have been preaching the word of the Lord. It is not because I'm preaching condemnation or legalism, but it is the mighty hand of an awesome **God**.

As the fear of the Lord came upon the congregation, I could no longer preach. I went to my office to lie on my face. After the service was completed, people came and told me that many of those present stood up and confessed their sins. No one had encouraged them to do this. The **Spirit** of **God** was upon them in such a mighty way that they could not help themselves. When true revival comes, you will see many of those who confess they wanted revival, running to preserve their fleshly lives.

During this time, the church went through a time of great purging and cleansing. But we discovered very quickly that we did not have a very solid foundation. People could not deal with the convicting power of **God**. Many of them had never experienced the fear of the Lord before.

Paul, the Apostle, declared, **knowing the terror of the Lord we persuade men**! He also declared, **working out your salvation with fear and trembling for it is God which worketh in you both to will and to do of his good pleasure**. **God** was calling us into his image and likeness, to be **Holy** as He is **Holy**! But the process is too painful for many of those who claim to love and to know **CHRIST**.

They Smelt & Felt the Horrors of HELL!

In the past, as I had shared in meetings just small portions of what I experienced when **God** took me to hell, there have been those who have begun to experience the smells, sounds, torments, and pains of this terrible and terrifying place; physically, mentally, and emotionally.

In one of these situations, there was a minister's wife whom I had known for a significant length of time. For some unknown reason, she had approached me on numerous occasions in the past, trying to convince me that it was not necessary for **God** to give such an encounter to His people. I did not argue with her or try to persuade her either way. I have never tried to create or bring about a situation where someone would experience the agonies and torments of hell as I did. I would not wish this on anyone.

This minister and his wife were in a tent revival meeting I was conducting in Chambersburg, Pennsylvania. In this meeting, the Lord inspired me to speak a little along this line about the pains, sufferings, and agonies of eternal damnation. As I was speaking about hell, this sister in the Lord fell out of her chair to the sawdust-covered ground. She began to squirm, twist, scream, and wail in the most dreadful way.

It was the most heartbreaking and terrible weeping, moaning, and crying you could ever imagine. She continued in this fashion it seemed for over half an hour. When she was finally able to get her breath and talk, she shared with us in tears and horror what she had experienced. It was not the physical torments of hell that she had experienced. She told us that she had felt the absolute utter hopelessness and total lack of love in this terrible place. After this experience, she will now tell you that she now understands to some extent what I had experienced and still have been since 1975.

In another meeting in Wisconsin Dells, Wisconsin, I was speaking to an Indian tribe called the Ho-Chunk Nation. They had contacted me after one of their leaders read my book "The Horrors of Hell & the Splendors of Heaven." They wanted me to come and speak to their tribe because of the horrendous immorality, which was permeating their community.

The **Spirit**ual leaders of this tribe felt in their hearts that if the fear of the Lord came upon their tribe, their people might repent and get right with **God**. I felt in my heart that this was directed by the Lord. Never had I gone anywhere to speak specifically and nothing but the subject of hell.

I arrived at their reservation in June 2008. In the evening service, the **Holy Spirit** was evident by a tangible invisible **Holiness**. As I was sharing some of my experience as I went to hell, a young Indian girl turned to her mother and told her that she was smelling the worst smell she had ever smelled in her life. She said that her nostrils fulfilled with the smell of rotten eggs and suffocating sulfur. This is not something that's new.

It is reported that when Jonathan Edwards preached his famous sermon "Sinners in the Hands of an Angry **God**" that those in the meeting could feel the flames of hell licking at their feet. Some reported it almost felt as if they were falling through the rotten canvas. They could hear the screams and the cries of those in hell. They held on to the front church pews so intensely that their fingers turned chalk white. Out of that meeting came a tremendous revival. The Apostle Paul was constantly warning the church about its eternal destiny. He told the body to work out its salvation with fear and trembling.

"Wherefore, my beloved, as ye have always obeyed, not as in my presence only, but now much more in my absence, work out your salvation with fear and trembling" (Phil. 2:12).

The church of the twenty-first century has lost the understanding that we absolutely need supernatural encounters with the presence of the Lord. From Genesis to Revelation, we see encounter after encounter of men and women with the **Divine** supernatural. It is by supernatural **Visitations** and visions that **God** reveals Himself and His will for humanity. It is also by these **Divine Visitations** that He transforms, molds, and shapes His people for a specific task, even as the potter does the clay. The revelation that we have of the Word of **God** was given by **Divine** Encounter.

Revival at the Huntington County Fair

My vacation time was coming up as a pastor, and I had two weeks in the summertime. The **Spirit** of **God** had spoken to my heart, prophetically to put a tent up at the Huntington County Fair. I began to investigate where I could get a tent. I was informed that another **Christ**ian group had a campground in Roxbury, Pennsylvania, and they would rent you a tent for a very good price. I could reach them and gave them the dates I wanted to rent their tent. I decided to pick the rental tent up. The tent I was going to rent would seat two hundred people.

Next, I contacted people in Huntington to find out who the coordinator of the Huntington Fair was. When I finally got his number, I called him up. He informed me all the spaces were filled in advance for two years ahead of time. I was not worried because it wasn't my responsibility to make it happen. If I had truly heard from **God**, then all I had to do was my part, **God** would do the rest. I did not tell this person that they had to give me a place because **God** told me.

I simply asked him to speak to the personnel who made these decisions. When he came back, he said they had an empty space they always kept open for people who wanted to have picnics. It was right next to the **FIRE** department's bingo stand. They said if we wanted to put up a gospel tent we could use that area. Praise **God** for His favour! **God** did awesome things under that tent.

The Lord's hand was on these tent meetings in the Huntington Fair. People came to me, wanting to be involved. **God** lined up some tremendous **Holy** Ghost preachers and singers. About 1/6 of the tent was used for a prayer area. I used tent curtains and strung them across behind a platform where people could pray before, during, and after the services in privacy.

We planned to conduct services in the afternoon and evening. It would be just a week long. People began to gather in the mornings to pray, including a good minister friend of mine. He moved in gifts of the **Holy** Ghost in a wonderful way. As we were in prayer, the Lord quickened to my heart that the **Holy** Ghost was about to show Himself in unusual ways—that people would even begin to fall under the power of the **Spirit** as they were walking past the tent. I informed the volunteer workers who were with us to get ready for this to happen.

As I was ministering in the afternoon session one day, the presence of **God** began to manifest Himself in a precious way. I looked out and saw an older lady crumpled to the ground about thirty feet in front of us. I pointed her out to the workers in the tent. They ran out and brought her in. There was nothing physically wrong with her as far as we could tell. She did not understand what was happening to her, but the **Spirit** of **God** was convicting her heart to such an extent that she gave her life to **JESUS** on the spot and was wonderfully saved.

That was the beginning of a wonderful move of **God** in Huntington. This tent meeting later helped give birth to a church of now over three hundred people.

Then a cloud covered the tent of the congregation, and the glory of the LORD filled the tabernacle (Exodus 40:34).

Philippians 4:7 And the peace of God, which passeth all understanding, shall keep your hearts and minds through Christ Jesus.

CHAPTER THREE

We As Believers Are To Be Gods SHOFAR

We need to understand that **God** desires to speak through us.

2 Peter 1:21 For the prophecy came not in old time by the will of man: but holy men of God spake as they were moved by the

Holy Ghost.

God knew all of this before he made everything. He made us with this in his heart and mind. In Zechariah, it reveals that **God** himself blows the **TRUMPET**. As we are speaking underneath the inspiration of the **Spirit**, it is the **Spirit** speaking out of our vocal cords.

John, the Baptist, was the **TRUMPET** of **God** sounding forth supernatural to prepare the way for Christ.

Matthew 3:2 and saying, Repent ye: for the kingdom of heaven is at hand. 3 For this is he that was spoken of by the prophet Esaias, saying, The Voice of one crying in the wilderness, Prepare ye the way of the Lord, make his paths straight. 4 And the same John had his raiment of camel's hair, and a leathern girdle about his loins; and his meat was locusts and wild honey.

Great Awakening

In the great awakening, during the time of Wesley, there were no buildings big enough to house all of the people. John Wesley, in Great Britain, would stand on the side of a hill where tens of thousands would gather to hear him preach, and it was the same for George Whitfield. Their **Voice**s were supernaturally empowered by the **Spirit** of **God** to when you could hear every word they spoke without a PA system. It was a Divine and supernatural Grace that the Lord used through them. How come **God** used them in this way? I believe it is because they pressed into **God**.

I know what's going on in the body of Christ at this present moment. We're not pressing into **God** like they did in Wesley and Whitfield's day. It is not just people to spend hours in prayer, but it is a faith that they are exercising while they are praying. We must believe that **God** hears our prayers because we are praying the will of the **Father**. We are not praying some kind of Mickey Mouse, Donald Duck, and self-centered prayer.

We are crying out, Oh **God**, let Christ be exalted. May **Jesus** be glorified. Lord, break the bands of the wicked. Drive out the darkness, Lord. Lord, we ask you to send the Holy Ghost rain. **God,** in his word, tells us that we must ask for the early and the latter rain and He will send it.

Our prayers are not based upon feelings or emotions, but it is faith, trust, confidence in **God** and His word. Many believers that I have known through the years have questioned whether or not **God** loved them? Since February 19, 75, February 18th, I have never questioned **God**'s love for me. How do you know he loves you? He showed it when the **Father** spared not his own son. **Jesus** hanging upon the cross is the eternal, ultimate evidence of his love for those who have surrendered their lives to him.

Romans 8:32 He that spared not his own Son, but delivered him up for us all, how shall he not with him also freely give us all things?

If you're ever going to have strong faith, you must realize deep within your heart that God cannot lie. The foundation of all sin is built upon the lie that the serpent spoke to the woman when he insinuated that **God** doesn't mean what he said. He told the woman that she would not die, even though **God** said she would.

That's the foundation of all unbelief. Did you hear that? We were created in faith by faith that the triune **God**head had in themselves.

2 Timothy 2:13 if we believe not, yet he abideth faithful: he cannot deny himself.

God created man in the midst of a Celestial war that was taking place in the heavenly's. This war was between Michael and his angels, and Lucifer and his angels. Lucifer succeeded in getting one-third of the angelic host to follow him in rebellion against **God**.

Revelation 12:7 And there was war in heaven: Michael and his angels fought against the dragon, and the dragon fought and his angels,

The human race was created in this time of war. Please get this deep into your heart **God** created us for war. We are made to be instruments of war in the hands of **God**. One of the main purposes of the **TRUMPET** was to sound the alarm. Wake up the people. It was for battle. They always used the **SHOFAR** during the time of battle.

How about around Jericho? How about in the time of Gideon when is 300 men broke the gourds that had flames of **FIRE** in them. Then they blew their **TRUMPET**s. These **TRUMPET**s were made from the **HORN**s of the Rams of male sheep.

Judges 7:17 And he said unto them, Look on me, and do likewise: and, behold, when I come to the outside of the camp, it shall be that, as I do, so shall ye do. 18 When I blow with a TRUMPET, I and all that are with me, then blow ye the TRUMPETs also on every side of all the camp, and say, The sword of the Lord, and of Gideon.

19 So Gideon, and the hundred men that were with him, came unto the outside of the camp in the beginning of the middle watch; and they had but newly set the watch: and they blew the TRUMPETs, and brake the pitchers that were in their hands.

God wants to use you like a **TRUMPET**. He wants you to be a sanctified **SHOFAR** that His wind can blow through you. The ram's **HORN** must be hollowed out. As the wind of the **Spirit** blows through you, mighty deeds, victories, battles will be won. Just like when the walls of Jericho fell flat.

Just like the enemies of Israel in Gideon turned on each other, bringing about their total destruction. You can bowl when through that no obstructions. And it just came into my heart and I began to study. And so I began to investigate. And the very first thing I discovered that before they would take a Ram's **HORN**, and throughout the Bible,

The Substance of the SHOFAR

The **SHOFAR** may be the **HORN** of any animal, except that of a cow or calf, in deference to the biblical golden calf incident. Traditionally, the preferred **HORN** is that of a ram. Some rabbinical authorities hold that the **HORN** can even be made from a non-kosher animal.

Bovine **HORN**s are made of keratin, the same material which forms the human toenail or fingernail. An antler, on the other hand, is not a **HORN** but solid bone. Such antlers are not used for **SHOFAR**s because they cannot be hollowed.

The Elef Hamagan (586:5) delineates the order of preference: 1) Curved ram's **HORN**, 2) curved **HORN** of other types of sheep, 3) curved **HORN** of other animals, 4) straight ram's or other kosher animal's **HORN** 5) the **HORN** of a non-kosher animal 6) cow **HORN**. (from the internet)

THE MAKING OF THE SHOFAR

We need to understand this process, the transformation of a Ram's **HORN** into a Beautiful instrument called a **SHOFAR**! By the way, you are reading this book by Divine Appointment. We will now go through the important 14 steps to becoming a **SHOFAR** for **God**.

The purpose of this whole book was to bring you to this point. We are to be the glorious **TRUMPETs** through which the wind of the **Spirit** is declaring with a **THUNDER**ous **VOICE** the everlasting gospel. This is a process that is directed by the **Divine** influence of **God himself**. This process of transforming a dead, stinky, ugly, useless **RAM**'s **HORN** into a beautiful **TRUMPET** use to take an expert **Craftsman** three months of hard work to complete. Of course, now with modern technology and equipment, they can accomplish this in a matter of days.

Numbers 10:1 And the Lord spake unto Moses, saying,
2 Make thee two TRUMPETs of silver; of a whole piece shalt thou make them: that thou mayest use them for the calling of the assembly, and for the journeying of the camps.
3 And when they shall blow with them, all the assembly shall assemble themselves to thee at the door of the tabernacle of the

congregation.
4 And if they blow but with one TRUMPET, then the princes, which are heads of the thousands of Israel, shall gather themselves unto thee.
5 When ye blow an alarm, then the camps that lie on the east parts shall go forward.
6 When ye blow an alarm the second time, then the camps that lie on the south side shall take their journey: they shall blow an alarm for their journeys.
7 But when the congregation is to be gathered together, ye shall blow, but ye shall not sound an alarm.
8 And the sons of Aaron, the priests, shall blow with the TRUMPETs; and they shall be to you for an ordinance forever throughout your generations.
9 And if ye go to war in your land against the enemy that oppresseth you, then ye shall blow an alarm with the TRUMPETs; and ye shall be remembered before the Lord your God, and ye shall be saved from your enemies.
10 Also in the day of your gladness, and in your solemn days, and in the beginnings of your months, ye shall blow with the TRUMPETs over your burnt offerings, and the sacrifices of your peace offerings; that they may be to you for a memorial before your God: I am the Lord your God.

God instructed Moses to make two **HORN**s out of silver. Yet we notice that the priest blew seven **HORN**s before the Ark of the Covenant. These **TRUMPET**s were made of the **HORN**s of **RAMS (male sheep)**. For these **RAMS HORN**s to be made usable, they had to go through a **14 Step Process**. I believe that this process is a graphic insight into what must happen in the life of a believer to be used as an instrument of righteousness in the kingdom of **God**.

Here are the 14 Steps we will be revealing

#1 Selection of the RAM
#2 Death of the RAM
#3 Breaking of the HORN
#4 The Bone Cartlidge Removed
#5 The Grinding of the HORN
#6 Placed into the FIRE
#7 HORN Is Straightened
#8 HORN is put In the Mold,
#9 HORN put under a stream of cold water
#10 Tip of HORN Is Cut off
#11 HORN has a Hole Drilled Through It
#12 In the FIRE Again
#13 HORN Is Fine Tuned
#14 Polished to the Glory Is Revealed

THE MAKING OF THE SHOFAR

#1 Selection of the RAM

In Genesis, after man sinned, we see **God** selecting sheep that he sacrificed to cover the nakedness of Adam and his wife. The next time we see a sacrificial animal, a sheep, was one able offered his best on to **God**. After the flood, Noah offered up to **God** a sacrificial lamb. When Abraham obeyed **God** by offering up his son Isaac, as he was getting to plunge the knife into his only begotten son, an angel of the Lord called out to him.

Genesis 22:12 And he said, Lay not thine hand upon the lad, neither do thou anything unto him: for now I know that thou fearest God, seeing thou hast not withheld thy son, thine only son from me.13 And Abraham lifted his eyes, and looked, and behold behind him a RAM caught in a thicket by his HORNs: and Abraham went and took the RAM, and offered him up for a burnt offering in the stead of his son.14 And Abraham called the name of that place Jehovahjireh: as it is said to this day, In the mount of the Lord it shall be seen.

God himself chose a **RAM** to take the place of Isaac, the son of Abraham. This **RAM** was a type and a shadow of the sacrificial death of **JESUS CHRIST**. **God** himself offered up his son for our redemption and atonement for sins. In Exodus, Moses was instructed to find a Lamb without spot or blemish. It had to be a male lamb that was the firstborn of its mother. Once again, this is a declaration of **CHRIST**.

Exodus 12:21 Then Moses called for all the elders of Israel, and said unto them, Draw out and take you a lamb according to your families, and kill the Passover.

The RAM's HORN Represents CHRIST and the Believer

Even as **God** chose the Passover Lamb through Moses, so he has chosen and known us before the foundation of the world.

Ephesians 1:4 According as he hath chosen us in him before the foundation of the world, that we should be Holy and without blame before him in love:

2 Timothy 1:9 Who hath saved us, and called us with an Holy calling, not according to our works, but according to his own purpose and grace, which was given us in CHRIST JESUS before the world began,

JESUS declared that in less the FATHER draws us, we will not come to him!

John 6:44 No man can come to me, except the FATHER which hath sent me draw him: and I will raise him up at the last day.

John 6:65 And he said, Therefore said I unto you, that no man can come unto me, except it were given unto him of my FATHER.

Jeremiah 31:3 The Lord hath appeared of old unto me, saying, Yea, I have loved thee with an everlasting love: therefore with lovingkindness have I drawn thee.

The very first step is that **God** Called you, and you responded. **Many are called, but few are chosen**. You have a hunger for **Spirit**ual truth, and that is why you are reading this book. It means you've been chosen, but you're still useless when you first get born again to a great extent, but you are chosen so ay it: I am chosen.

If you have been drawn to God, it is because his Spirit has Chosen You!

***John 15:16 Ye have not chosen me, but I have chosen you, and ordained you, that ye should go and bring forth fruit, and that your fruit should remain:**

1 Corinthians 1:27 But God hath chosen the foolish things of the world to confound the wise; and God hath chosen the weak things of the world to confound the things which are mighty;

James 2:5 Hearken, my beloved brethren, Hath not God chosen the poor of this world rich in faith, and heirs of the kingdom which he hath promised to them that love him?
We see this when it comes to the Prophets of the old, and the Fivefold of the new!

Jeremiah 1:5 Before I formed thee in the belly I knew thee; and before thou camest forth out of the womb I sanctified thee, and I ordained thee a prophet unto the nations. (Jeremiah the prophet)

Galatians 1:15 But when it pleased God, who separated me from my mother's womb, and called me by his grace, (Paul the apostle)
Matthew 22:14 For many are called, but few are chosen.

Revelation 3:20 Behold, I stand at the door, and knock: if any man hear my VOICE, and open the door, I will come in to him, and will sup with him, and he with me.

1 Peter 2:9 - But ye [are] a chosen generation, a royal

priesthood, an holy nation, a peculiar people; that ye should shew forth the praises of him who hath called you out of darkness into his marvellous light:

Jeremiah 1:5 - Before I formed thee in the belly I knew thee; and before thou camest forth out of the womb I sanctified thee, [and] I ordained thee a prophet unto the nations.

Ephesians 1:4 according as he hath chosen us in him before the foundation of the world, that we should be holy and without blame before him in love:

Deuteronomy 14:2 - For thou [art] an holy people unto the LORD thy God, and the LORD hath chosen thee to be a peculiar people unto himself, above all the nations that [are] upon the earth.

2 Thessalonians 2:14 - Whereunto he called you by our gospel, to the obtaining of the glory of our Lord Jesus Christ.

If You Have responded to the Gospel, with conviction and hunger, you are chosen!

My Amazing Supernatural Salvation

Becoming The Lord's SHOFAR

It was my nineteenth birthday (February 18, 1975). I was in the Navy at the time and heavily involved in alcohol, drugs, and other un**God**ly activities. I had decided to commit suicide. I do not remember anyone ever sharing the gospel of **JESUS CHRIST** with me. No one ever took the time to warn me about eternal damnation for those who did not know **God**.

Even to this day, it amazes me that the government ever accepted me into the Navy (back in 1973 when I was 17 years old). At the time, I had major mental, emotional, and even physical problems, which included hearing problems and a major speech impediment. I quit school at 15 years old, leaving home until I ended up in trouble with the law at 16.

I was given the option of being prosecuted or joining the military. I chose the military. However, for the military to accept me, I had to have my GED. Subsequently, I worked extremely hard to get it, and I succeeded. At the time, I believed that joining the Navy would take me out of the drugs, violence, immorality, and alcohol lifestyle that I had been living. That could not have been farther from the truth.

As soon as I graduated from basic training, Uncle Sam shipped me to San Diego, California, for further training on repairing 16mm projectors. Upon accomplishing this training, I was sent to Adak, Alaska, in the Aleutian Islands. I was assigned to the special services department. They provided all of the entertainment for the men on base. This included the movie theater, bowling alley, roller-skating rink, horse stables for taking men hunting and the cafeteria (not the chow hall).

I was extremely unreliable and incompetent, so much so that within the two years that I was there, I was transferred to every one of those facilities. My last job ended up being at the horse stables shoveling manure. During this time, I was heavily involved in drugs, including selling them.

I was drinking a lot of alcohol, including ripple wine, vodka, and tequila. I smoked an average of 3 1/2 packs of cigarettes per day, not including cigars. I used Brown Mule, Copenhagen, Beach Nut, and Skoal chewing tobaccos. My favorite singing groups were Dr. Hook and the Medicine Band, Pink Floyd, The Grateful Dead, and America.

When I was off duty, my attire was extremely strange. First off, when I was younger, my older brother knocked out my front tooth. Of course, I had it replaced with a pegged tooth, but while I was stationed in Adak, it got knocked out again. Thus, I picked up a ridiculous nickname. I was called "Tooth."

I wanted to fit in with the cowboy crowd, so I found an old cowboy hat which was too large for me. To make it fit, I took an old military ski hat and sewed it on the inside so that it would be snug on my head. (Of course, this old Stetson cowboy hat was too large for me.) As I would walk around the base with this large cowboy hat, it would be flopping on top of my head, making me look extremely silly; especially with me missing one of my front teeth.

I did not want just to be a cowboy because I was also a hippie. So, with a bright new idea, I went to the cafeteria and asked for all of their chicken necks. I took these chicken necks and boiled them in a pot of hot vinegar water. Then I took these chicken bones after they were cleaned and strung them on a leather strand. I would wear these chicken bones as a necklace around my neck. It really stank! No wonder I was extremely depressed all the time. I think that you can begin to see what kind of a mess I was.

On my 19th birthday, I was overwhelmed with self-pity and depression. I decided to end it all by slitting my wrist! I went into the bathroom with a large, survival hunting knife. I put the knife to my wrist with full intentions of slitting my artery. I was determined to kill myself. I held the knife firmly against my wrist and took one more last breath before I slid it across my wrist.

Suddenly, an invisible presence came rushing down upon me like a blanket. It was a tangible, overwhelming presence of mind-boggling fear. It was the fear of **God**, and it overwhelmed me! Instantly, I realized with the crystal-clear understanding that I was going to hell. I deserved hell; I belonged in hell, and hell had a right to me. Furthermore, I knew if I slit my wrist, I would be in hell forever.

Overwhelming Love

I walked out of that little military bathroom to my bunk. I fell on my knees, reached my hands up toward heaven, and cried out to **JESUS** with all of my heart. All of this was supernatural and strange. I did not ever recall any time when anyone ever shared with me how to become a **Christ**ian or how to be converted. I knew how to pray. I cried out to **JESUS** and told Him I believed He was the Son of **God**, had been raised from the dead, and I desperately needed Him. I not only asked Him into my heart, but I gave Him my heart, soul, mind, and life.

At that very instant, a love beyond description came rushing into my heart. I knew what love was for the first time in my life. At the same time, I comprehended what I was placed on this earth for—I was here to follow, love, serve, and obey **God**. Deep love and hunger to know **God** grabbed my heart. I was filled with love from top to bottom, inside and out—inexpressibly unbelievable. **JESUS** had come to live inside of me!

Instantaneous Deliverance

I was instantly delivered: from over three packs of cigarettes a day, from worldly and satanic music, from chewing tobacco; from cussing and swearing, from drugs and alcohol, and from a filthy and dirty mind.

Some might ask why my conversion was so **dramatic**. I believe that it's because I had nothing to lose. I knew down deep that there was not one single thing worth saving in me. The only natural talent I ever possessed was the ability to mess things up. At the time of my salvation, I completely surrendered my heart and life to **JESUS CHRIST**.

THE MAKING OF THE SHOFAR

#2 Death of the RAM

The choosing of the **RAM** is just the beginning of the process.

There must now be a surrendering, a yielding, submitting, believing, and trusting in the Savior. Up to this time, this **RAM** is still alive. It will not be yielded and surrender to **God** until it is offered as a personal sacrifice of its own free will.

Of course, I am talking about the life of a believer who must become a living sacrifice to **God**. Alive unto **God**, but dead to the world. It goes back to the very first prayer that **CHRIST** taught his disciples.

Luke 11:2 And he said unto them, When ye pray, say, Our FATHER which art in heaven, Hallowed be thy name. Thy kingdom come. Thy will be done, as in heaven, so in earth.

This is the most basic and elementary step into being prepared to be an instrument in the hands of **God**. You will never go very far **Spirit**ually until this heart of wanting to surrender to nothing but the will of **God** is leading and guiding you.

JESUS CHRIST has been given as our supreme example when it comes to surrendering to the perfect will of **God**. He became our sacrifice, not seeking his own will, but the will of the **FATHER**. This is exemplified to us by the prayer that **CHRIST** prayed in the garden of Gethsemane.

Matthew 26:39 And he went a little farther, and fell on his face, and prayed, saying, O my FATHER, if it is possible, let this cup pass from me: nevertheless not as I will, but as thou wilt.

This was not an easy prayer to pray because of what **CHRIST** knew in his heart he was going to have to do. **He who knew no sin was going to be made sin for us.** He that had never been apart from his **FATHER before the beginning of time** would now be separated for three days and three nights. All the pains, the sufferings, the torments of the lost would be upon him. What **God** has asked us to sacrifice, compared to what **CHRIST** is as nothing, compared to our reward throughout eternity.

Romans 8:18 For I reckon that the sufferings of this present time are not worthy to be compared with the glory which shall be revealed in us.

Maybe you have been taught; since **JESUS CHRIST** suffered for us, we no longer must suffer. **This is wrong**. We get to partake of his glorious, wonderful, sufferings. We are permitted to become partakers of his pain and his agony in saying **NO to the world, the flesh, and the devil**.

We can now boldly shout, and declare, **YES to God, and His WILL to be done in our lives**. Paul said we must go through much tribulation to enter into the kingdom of heaven. This is not talking about being born again, but entering into a realm where all things are possible.

Galatians 2:19 For I through the law am dead to the law, that I might live unto God.20 I am crucified with CHRIST: nevertheless I live; yet not I, but CHRIST liveth in me: and the life which I now live in the flesh I live by the faith of the Son of God, who loved me, and gave himself for me.

There will be many times in your life when **God** gives you the opportunity to die to self. He might even ask you to lay down your life as a martyr for the sake of the kingdom, and for the salvation of others. I have experienced this at times in my **Spirit**ual walk with **God**. Many times, I did not know if I was going to survive a certain task He laid upon my heart. Here is an example of one such test of love, faith, and obedience to the will of **God**.

God Asked Me: Will you die for me? (1994)

I heard the **VOICE** of **God** asking me: are you willing to die for me? It was as I was getting ready to leave for the Philippines. I had been to the Philippines on numerous occasions. I had been going into an area of the Philippines where the NPA was extremely active. NPA is the abbreviation for the new People's Army, which is part of a communist movement.

At that time, they were very active, and they were extremely brutal and dangerous. **God**ly men which I have worked with in the Philippines had been murdered by them. I heard the Lord continue to say to me: if I can use your spilled blood like a seed planted into the ground to bring about a wonderful harvest, are you willing to die? When I heard the Lord say this to me, I took it very seriously. With deep sorrow in my heart and tears rolling down my face, I said yes Lord!

It was not that I was not willing to die for **CHRIST** because I had been in many dangerous situations since I had been born again in 1975. I have had numerous encounters with people threatening and trying to kill me. A gang I used to run without of Chicago tried twice. Some Yupik Indians in Alaska had tried to kill me. A demon possessed woman had stabbed me multiple times in the face, and yet the knife could not penetrate my skin. A radical Muslim kept on wanting to shoot me, as he yelled and screamed in my face, with his finger ready to pull the trigger which would have sent me off into eternity, but the **Holy** Ghost restrained him.

Yes, I was more than willing to die, but in truth, I did not want to. I had a lovely wife, three sons and a beautiful little girl. But I said yes Lord if this is your will! I still remember that morning as I was getting ready to drive myself to the BWI Airport to catch a plane to the Philippines. I hugged my precious wife very tight and my four beautiful children as if it was like the last time I would ever hold them or hug them again on this side of heaven.

As I looked at my little girl Stephanie, she was sucking on her two fingers, and I had lovingly nicknamed her two fingers, Stephanie. My 2nd son Daniel I had nicknamed him the watermelon kid because he loved watermelon so much. I hugged my oldest son goodbye, who we had nicknamed Mick, which is short for Michael. My 3rd son Steven I could never give enough hugs to even to this day. He loves hugs!

As I backed out of my driveway, leaving my family standing on the front porch tears were rolling down my face. I said Lord you died for me, you gave everything for me, so the least I can do is to be willing to give up everything you've given me if I can be a seed of revival for others to be born again.

As I was driving towards the airport on the main highway, I was weeping so hard that I could barely see where I was going. I was thanking **God** for the years that he had given me with my lovely wife, Kathleen. I was thanking **God** for my three sons and my daughter. I was thanking **God** for all the opportunities he had given to me to minister the word and help others. I was also reflecting upon the fact of how many times I should have been dead like many of my former friends who were now dead.

I thought back on the times before I was born again when I had overdosed, drank too much booze, played chicken with oncoming trains, driving on the other side of the road headed right towards others, when I had been in a gunfight with a crazy man. Oh, how many times **God** had spared me, and yet most of my worldly friends were now dead.

All of those times, when **God** spared my life, he could've allowed me to die and go to hell. But **God** had rescued me, and now it was my turn to die for him, how could I say no? I remember landing in the Philippines. I was completely free from fear. In my heart of hearts, I was already a martyr for **CHRIST**.

Now to my wonderful amazement and my great surprise, **God** spoke to my heart while I was over there in the communist-infested area. He said: son, you're not going to die! I said what Lord? He spoke to me again: you're not going to die! I remember crying with joy; I said why, Lord? He said I needed to have you prove your love for me. He said I needed to have you to know that I was number 1 in your life. Even as Abraham offered up Isaac, and I gave him back, so in a sense, you have offered up your wife and your children, and I give them back to you.

That was over 20 years ago when the Lord spared my life. I'm still going to areas at times that are extremely dangerous, but I have no fear because I know that **God** is with me. What if he ever asked me to offer up my life again as a seed with the shedding of my blood? All I can say is that if it ever happens again, by **God**'s grace I'll say, yes Lord! You gave your life for me; it's the least I can do.

So the second thing that must happen to the Ram, it must die. If we are dead with Christ, we will live with him. If you are dead and risen, seek those things that are above.

There are many that are born again. They are **God**'s chosen people, but they just will not die to their flesh. They should have a heart, an attitude that says: **not my will, but Father your will be done**.

Please take notice: They never make a **TRUMPET** out of fresh killed Ram. When they sacrifice that Ram, they cut the head off. The head is thrown into a very dry atmosphere to where all the moisture dries up. All the FLESH falls off. Have you ever seen out in the desert the skull of a Long**HORN** cattle? They use it as symbolism for death.

Well, if you go on the Internet, you can have a profound visual experience of all that is involved in making a **SHOFAR**. I studied videos about how to make a **TRUMPET**. Some of the videos will show you piles of the heads of dead rams.

Now, they have to use a kosher animal

Which Animals Are Kosher? The Torah enjoins Jewish people to eat only certain animals, which are commonly referred to as kosher. Which animals are kosher?

Land Animal

A land animal is kosher if it both

a) Has split hooves and

b) Chews its cud.

Examples of kosher animals include cows, **sheep**, goats, and deer. Examples of non-kosher animals include pigs, rabbits, squirrels, bears, dogs, cats, camels, and horses.

Note: All warm-blooded kosher creatures (mammals and birds) must also undergo shechitah (kosher slaughter) and salting (to remove blood) before being eaten. In practice, the only meat that is sold with reliable kosher certification may be used.

They can use a gazelle and other kosher animals, but they liked to use the **HORN**s of a ram. The head has to be completely dried out. That's a little bit of a process. How many know dying to self is a process?

Smith Wigglesworth, a plumber, mightily used of **God,** said this: **Smith - "Before God could bring me to this place He has BROKEN me a thousand times. I have wept, I have groaned, I have travailed many a night until God BROKE me. It seems to me that until God has mowed you down, you never can have this longsuffering for others. We can never have the gifts of healing and the working of miracles in operation only as we stand in the divine power that God gives us and we stand believing God, and having done all we still stand believing."**

Some people can die very quick. They just abandoned themselves to **God**. Many people yes to **God**, and then they take back their commitment! Now, once the head, the skull, and the **HORN**s are sufficiently dried out, that means there's no life in them, it is ready for the next step.

Galatians 2:20 - I am crucified with Christ: nevertheless I live; yet not I, but Christ liveth in me: and the life which I now live in the flesh I live by the faith of the Son of God, who loved me, and gave himself for me.

Luke 9:23 - And he said to [them] all, If any [man] will come after me, let him deny himself, and take up his cross daily, and follow me.

Galatians 5:24 - And they that are Christ's have crucified the flesh with the affections and lusts.

Mark 8:35 - For whosoever will save his life shall lose it; but whosoever shall lose his life for my sake and the gospel's, the same shall save it.

John 12:24 - Verily, verily, I say unto you, Except a corn of wheat fall into the ground and die, it abideth alone: but if it die, it bringeth forth much fruit.

Romans 6:1-23 - What shall we say then? Shall we continue in sin, that grace may abound? (Read More...)

Matthew 10:38 - And he that taketh not his cross, and followeth after me, is not worthy of me.

Philippians 2:1-30 - If [there be] therefore any consolation in Christ, if any comfort of love, if any fellowship of the Spirit, if any bowels and mercies, (Read More...)

1 Corinthians 15:31 - I protest by your rejoicing which I have in Christ Jesus our Lord, I die daily.

1 Peter 2:24 - Who his own self bare our sins in his own body on the tree, that we, being dead to sins, should live unto righteousness: by whose stripes ye were healed.

1 Peter 4:1-11 - Forasmuch then as Christ hath suffered for us in the flesh, arm yourselves likewise with the same mind: for he that hath suffered in the flesh hath ceased from sin; (Read More...)

Colossians 3:3 - For ye are dead, and your life is hid with Christ in God.

Romans 12:1 - I beseech you therefore, brethren, by the mercies of God, that ye present your bodies a living sacrifice, holy, acceptable unto God, [which is] your reasonable service.

2 Corinthians 5:17 - Therefore if any man [be] in Christ, [he is] a new creature: old things are passed away; behold, all things are become new.

2 Corinthians 4:8 - [We are] troubled on every side, yet not distressed; [we are] perplexed, but not in despair;

Philippians 1:21 - For to me to live [is] Christ, and to die [is] gain.

CHAPTER FOUR

THE MAKING OF THE SHOFAR

The Initial Sorting

The HORNs are bought in bulk – by tons and are shipped to Israel by sea. The HORNs arrive in their natural form, as they were on the beast's head. The HORN's cover is rough and lacks shine, and the HORN's bone is still inside it.

There is a lot of waste in HORNs, any crack or break disqualifies the SHOFAR. Most HORNs arrive cracked, and some of them are even rotten. A mere thirty percent of the HORNs reach the stage of processing, and any scratch in the process of making counts, since it may crack the HORN and be wasted.

SHOFAR makers make a point of receiving strong HORNs, at least half a meter long, because also during production there is considerable wear and tear. Each HORN weighs approximately 1-2 kg. (From the Internet)

#3 Breaking of the HORN

If you'd like to know more about the process of turning a **RAM**'s **HORN** into an amazing **TRUMPET**, you can find numerous videos on YouTube. As I watched these videos, I was amazed at the process, which needs to be **Spirit**ually applied to a believer's life. After the **RAM**, has been slain, they take the head and simply put it into a very dry atmosphere.

They allow this head to dry up. When it is completely dried, and all the flesh has rotted away, it looks like a long**HORN** steer found out in the desert of Arizona or Texas. You have the skull with the two **HORN**s sticking out of the head. This is how the **RAMS** head looks, with the two **HORN**s sticking out on either side. I think there are numerous **Spirit**ual applications to this condition.

Now the **HORN** on a **RAM** is its authority and power. This is not only true with the **RAM**, but with all animals that produce **HORN**s on their heads. With these **HORN**s, they exercise their dominant traits. **HORN**s are provided as defense from predators, tools in fighting other animals and including members of its species for territory or mating, feeding, courtship displays.

When I lived in Alaska back in the mid-70s, I saw **Moose**, and Caribou with very large **HORN**s, antlers. These **HORN**s, antlers made them extremely dangerous. With these **HORN**s, they could easily kill a human being. While I was there, I heard about a man who had bought a brand-new heavy-duty pickup truck. He had it all decked out with large tires, roll bars, and front crash bars on the bumper. He thought surely that his truck was almost invincible. He found out quickly that he was wrong.

One day he was driving down a road when he noticed up to a head a very large Bull Moose on the side of the road. He slowed up as he pulled up to this larger Moose, with a very large set of **HORN**s on its head. He thought he could just drive past this Moose, with no problems. Oh, was he so wrong!

As he drove past this Bull Moose, the Moose decided to attack the truck. He **rammed** it over and over with his large **HORN**s, his antlers on his head. He completely totaled this man's new truck, eventually flipping it over on its side. Without the **HORN**s, the antlers on this Moose it would not have been possible.

I believe these **HORN**s represent the macho-ism of a person, whether they be man or woman. This, **I can do it, kind of attitude**. It reminds me of Peter and his arrogance with the Lord. I will never betray you **JESUS**! Even when **JESUS** said to Peter - do you love me? You can hear the pride in his response -you know I love you, Lord. The Lord finally said to him that when he was older others would lead him about.

John 21:17 He saith unto him the third time, Simon, son of Jonas, lovest thou me? Peter was grieved because he said unto him the third time, Lovest thou me? And he said unto him, Lord, thou knowest all things; thou knowest that I love thee. JESUS saith unto him, Feed my sheep.

18 Verily, verily, I say unto thee, When thou wast young, thou girdest thyself, and walkedst whither thou wouldest: but when

thou shalt be old, thou shalt stretch forth thy hands, and another shall gird thee, and carry thee whither thou wouldest not.

Now, after a process of time, these **HORN**s on the dead, dry **RAMS** skulls were useless. They could be easily broken off. The **Craftsman** would examine the skulls to make sure that they had been dried sufficiently. He put the skull under his arm, in his armpit. Then he would take his hand, grabbing the **HORN**, and with a quick snap, he would break it off the skull. There are several **Spirit**ual principles involved in this.

#1 First, there must be separating from natural thinking.

No longer is the **HORN** attached to the head of the **RAM**. This is where many believers are snared. After they are born again, they keep leaning to the understanding of their natural mind. They keep trusting in their ability to work things out. There must now be a change in our thinking!

Isaiah 55:8 For my thoughts are not your thoughts, neither are your ways my ways, saith the Lord.9 For as the heavens are higher than the earth, so are my ways higher than your ways, and my thoughts than your thoughts.10 For as the rain cometh down, and the snow from heaven, and returneth not thither, but watereth the earth, and maketh it bring forth and bud, that it may give seed to the sower, and bread to the eater:11 So shall my word be that goeth forth out of my mouth: it shall not return unto me void, but it shall accomplish that which I please, and it shall prosper in the thing whereto I sent it.

Proverbs 3:5 Trust in the Lord with all thine heart; and lean not unto thine own understanding. 6 In all thy ways acknowledge him, and he shall direct thy paths.7 Be not wise in thine own eyes: fear the Lord, and depart from evil.8 It shall be health to thy navel, and marrow to thy bones.

Proverbs 28:26 He that trusteth in his own heart is a fool: but whoso walketh wisely, he shall be delivered.

Jeremiah 10:23 O Lord, I know that the way of man is not in himself: it is not in man that walketh to direct his steps.

Romans 12:2 - And be not conformed to this world: but be ye transformed by the renewing of your mind, that ye may prove what [is] that good, and acceptable, and perfect, will of God.

Philippians 4:8 - Finally, brethren, whatsoever things are true, whatsoever things [are] honest, whatsoever things [are] just, whatsoever things [are] pure, whatsoever things [are] lovely, whatsoever things [are] of good report; if [there be] any virtue, and if [there be] any praise, think on these things.

Romans 12:1-2 - I beseech you therefore, brethren, by the mercies of God, that ye present your bodies a living sacrifice, holy, acceptable unto God, [which is] your reasonable service. (Read More...)

Ephesians 4:23 - And be renewed in the Spirit of your mind;

1 Peter 1:13 - Wherefore gird up the loins of your mind, be sober, and hope to the end for the grace that is to be brought unto you at the revelation of Jesus Christ;

2 Corinthians 10:4-5 - (For the weapons of our warfare [are] not carnal, but mighty through God to the pulling down of strong holds;) (Read More...)

Colossians 3:2 - Set your affection on things above, not on things on the earth.

John 8:32 - And ye shall know the truth, and the truth shall make you free.

Philippians 2:5 - Let this mind be in you, which was also in Christ Jesus:

1 Corinthians 2:16 - For who hath known the mind of the Lord, that he may instruct him? But we have the mind of Christ.

#B Second there must no longer be any confidence in the flesh!

Today many are being taught that you must believe in yourself. This is what we would call humanism. Humanism is a philosophy of thought that emphasizes human values, capacities, and worth. It is the deification of the natural man and his abilities. It can be directly linked to the satanic teaching of evolution! Paul, the apostle, boldly declared that we are those (believers) who have no confidence in the flesh. We are not here to exalt ourselves, but to exalt **JESUS CHRIST**. The works of the flesh profit nothing!

Philippians 3:3 For we are the circumcision, which worship God in the Spirit, and rejoice in CHRIST JESUS, and have no confidence in the flesh.4 Though I might also have confidence in the flesh. If any other man thinketh that he hath whereof he might trust in the flesh, I more:5 Circumcised the eighth day, of the stock of Israel, of the tribe of Benjamin, an Hebrew of the Hebrews; as touching the law, a Pharisee;

Jeremiah 9:23 Thus saith the Lord, Let not the wise man glory in his wisdom, neither let the mighty man glory in his might, let not the rich man glory in his riches:

Psalm 125:1They that trust in the Lord shall be as mount Zion, which cannot be removed, but abideth forever.

#C Third A Radical Taking of an Ax

to All Worldly Indoctrination!

Luke 3:9 And now also the axe is laid unto the root of the trees: every tree therefore which bringeth not forth good fruit is hewn down, and cast into the FIRE.

2 Corinthians 10:4 (For the weapons of our warfare are not carnal, but mighty through God to the pulling down of strong holds;)5 Casting down imaginations, and every high thing that exalteth itself against the knowledge of God, and bringing into captivity every thought to the obedience of CHRIST;

Jeremiah 1:10 See, I have this day set thee over the nations and over the kingdoms, to root out, and to pull down, and to destroy, and to throw down, to build, and to plant.

The **HORN** must be broke off of the skull of the dead **RAM** in order for it to be turned into a majestic, beautiful, amazing **TRUMPET**, to be used for the glory of **God**'s kingdom.

EXPERIENCED A DEEP MOVE of the SPIRIT!

We were preparing to leave the church that we had been pastoring for two years. Because the church was bringing in new candidates for examination, they did not need me to preach the Word to them any longer.

Thus, I could spend many hours praying, memorizing, and meditating on Scriptures, talking to the Lord. I would walk the mountain that was behind our parsonage for hours on end every day just fellowshipping with **God**. This fellowship continued for several weeks. At the time, I did not realize that I was about to step into a much deeper realm of the **Spirit**.

I was going through a process of renewing my mind and being separated from my old way of thinking. My mind was coming into agreement with **God**'s word with my heart. **Amos 3: 3** says **-can two walk together except they be agreed?** Without realizing it, I was beginning to walk with **God** to the place where he could manifest himself as a minister for him.

My wife and I were scheduled to minister at several meetings, and I had been invited previously to minister at the Mifflin Full Gospel Businessmen's meeting located in Belleville, Pennsylvania. We arrived right before the meeting was to start. As I sat at a table with my wife, I remember that I felt no particular quickening of the **Spirit** of **God** on the inside whatsoever. One of the members of the organization came over and asked me if I would like to pray with some of the members before the beginning of the meeting. I consented to do so.

They were all standing in a circle holding each other's hands. I simply stepped into this circle and took the hand of the man on my right and left. The men began to pray, and I prayed very softly, agreeing with them. During this time of prayer, I did not perceive in my heart that I should pray aloud. When we were done praying, the man on my right hand, an older gentleman, stared at me. He said, "What in the world was that?"

I said to him, **"What do you mean?"**

He said it was like a streak of lightning came out of my hand, and up to his arm, through his face. You could tell that something radical had just taken place. I told him that I had not felt anything.

That was the beginning of an unusual night. This same gentleman came to me at the end of the service, crying. He asked me to consider his eyes. I still remember to this day; his eyes were clear blue and glistening. He said to me, "My eyes were covered in cataracts. I had not realized to later that the minute you touched me, cataracts melted right off my eyeballs!" **Thank you, JESUS!**

Right up to the minute before I opened my mouth to speak, I had not felt a single thing **Spirit**ually. However, the minute I began to talk, the rivers began to flow. I do not remember what exactly I said, but I do know I was speaking under a strong influence of the **Holy** Ghost. I flowed right into the gifts of the **Spirit** after the teaching of the Word. A very precise word of knowledge began to operate. I remember looking out over the people and beginning to call specific people out. Many of the women and men appeared to be Mennonite or Amish.

I began to point to specific people and call them to come forward. As they came, I would tell them by a word of knowledge what was going on in their bodies. When they would get within ten feet of me, they did not fall forward or backward, but just simply begin to crumple.

I have never seen anything like it! It was like they just simply, and very gently went down almost like a snowflake falling from the sky. As far as I know, all of them were instantly healed. I do not remember laying hands on anyone that night. The **FATHER**, the Son, and **Holy** Ghost were in the house.

THE MAKING OF THE SHOFAR

Separating the bone from the HORN's covering

After the initial sorting, a complex process begins in which the HORN's covering is separated from the bone inside it. The SHOFAR is made only from the HORN's covering. By the way, the HORN's covering is the same substance our fingernails are made of.

The separation is difficult, and it requires special skills not to break the SHOFAR. How is it done? Well, that is one of the profession's secrets! (From the Internet)

#4 The Bone Cartlidge Removed

The **RAM**'s **HORN** is still packed full of bone cartilage, which is sometimes called bone core. This soft bone cartilage runs from about two-thirds to the tip of the **HORN** all the way to its base where it was attached to the skull of the **RAM**.

For the **RAM**'s **HORN** to be turned into a **TRUMPET,** it must be **completely** hollowed out of this bone cartilage. Part of this process is accomplished in quite a unique way. They grab the **HORN** midway up towards the peak with one hand, and with the contrary, they hold a stick or a rubber mallet, and then they start **thumping and repeatedly hitting** it until the cartridge begins to break loose and fall out.

I think this is a fantastic illustration of what **God** must do with a yielded and hungry believer. Much of this process is accomplished by **God** by allowing us to go through **trials, test,** and **tribulations**. I am not saying that everything that happens to you is of **God**. Many times or I could say, most times; we are our own worst enemies. We open the door to be attacked by

#1 lack of faith,

#2 ignorance of knowledge,

#3 right out disobedience to God and his will.

There are times though that we are going through trials and test because we are smack dab in the middle of **God**'s will. **JESUS CHRIST** himself is a beautiful example of this fact. Not once, yes, not one time did **JESUS** ever step out of the will of his **FATHER**.

Hebrews 5:7 Who in the days of his flesh, when he had offered up prayers and supplications with strong crying and tears unto him that was able to save him from death, and was heard in that he feared;8 Though he were a Son, yet learned he obedience by the things which he suffered;9 And being made perfect, he became the author of eternal salvation unto all them that obey him;

King David made a surprising statement about his experiences.

Psalm 119:71 It is good for me that I have been afflicted; that I might learn thy statutes.

We may not like it, but **God** does bring chastisement to his people so that they might repent.

Psalm 119:67 Before I was afflicted I went astray: but now have I kept thy word.

Hebrews 12:10 For they verily for a few days chastened us after their own pleasure; but he for our profit, that we might be partakers of his Holiness.11 Now no chastening for the present seemeth to be joyous, but grievous: nevertheless afterward it yieldeth the peaceable fruit of righteousness unto them which are exercised thereby.

There must be an out with the old, and in with the **NEW**. The old bone cartilage is knocked out of the **RAMS HORN by a continual process of being thumped!** Then and **ONLY** then can it be filled with the sounds of heaven. When the conversion of this **HORN** is complete then will the mystical winds of the **Spirit** will fill this hollowed out portion of the **HORN**, bringing a **TRUMPET** blast that will echo over the mountains and the valleys with the loud declarations of the kingdom of heaven. The **THUNDERING** of Heaven will be heard in all of the 21 occasions previously mentioned!

Matthew 9:16 No man putteth a piece of new cloth unto an old garment, for that which is put in to fill it up taketh from the garment, and the rent is made worse.17 Neither do men put new wine into old bottles: else the bottles break, and the wine runneth out, and the bottles perish: but they put new wine into new bottles, and both are preserved.

1 Corinthians 5:7 Purge out therefore the old leaven, that ye

may be a new lump, as ye are unleavened. For even CHRIST our passover is sacrificed for us:

2 Corinthians 5:17 Therefore if any man be in CHRIST, he is a new creature: old things are passed away; behold, all things are become new.

Disqualified or Qualified (kosher)

After the covering is separated from the bone, the HORN is examined again to see if it qualifies for making a SHOFAR. Any HORN with a crack or hole penetrating into its inner part is disqualified.

If the hole or crack is superficial, the HORN is "kosher". No mending is performed because according to the written instructions the HORN must be "Hakol Mimino", i.e. – not having any foreign substance. Mending a SHOFAR using the same substance is very expensive, and it is done only in special cases, when a person is particularly attached to a certain SHOFAR, and is not prepared to give it up. (From the Internet)

I thought it was God, but it was the devil

(1984)

This is an imperative story I must tell. It may not seem important at first, but as you read this story, you'll discover that it is.

In the spring of 1984, I was hungry for **God**, wanting to draw closer to Him. To do this, I felt it was necessary for me to get alone with the Lord. So, I asked my wife if she would mind if I rented a room for a week at a rundown motel right down the road from our house; probably about a mile away. She said that would be all right with her, and besides, she could visit me anytime that she wanted. With my wife's blessing, I packed up a little suitcase of clothes, got in my car and drove down to the motel to rent a room.

After planning, I moved in. In the motel room, I had, there was a large TV which I did not want to watch. I unplugged it and turned the screen towards the wall. Then I sat down with my Bible, lexicons, concordances, and notepads and began to study and pray. During the coming week, I had determined that I was going to do nothing but pray, seek **God**'s face, fast, and deny my flesh.

My motive in this would seem to be right, but there was something a little distorted in this quest. You see, I wanted to hear the **VOICE** of **God**, very precisely and explicitly. Now, you might ask what's wrong with that. At the time, I did not realize it, but my motives were all wrong. Pride motivated me. If the great Dr. Mike Yeager could be used by **God** using the gifts of knowledge and wisdom, then people would be stunned with amazement; astounded and dumbfounded as to how **God** was using me.

You see, I had heard of and read about men that were so precise with their words of knowledge and wisdom that people would sit in complete and utter wonder at their abilities to know their problems and situations. I wanted what they had; all for the glory of **God** or so I told myself. But in all reality, my endeavor was all about me, me, me. This is such an easy trap to fall into: to believe that our goals are for the glory of **God** when, in all reality, it is for self.

During my 40 years of ministry plus, I have seen people fall into this very trap which had been set for me by the enemy of my soul. Many honestly believe that they are hearing the **VOICE** of **God** when, in fact, they are listening to familiar **Spirit**s. The doorway by which the enemy is coming in is through our hearts filled with pride.

I cannot tell you how many times that I had heard people say, "**God** told me" when it was no more **God** than there are green, polka-dotted men and black and white striped women living on the moon. I have heard people say, **God** told me to leave my husband, **God** told me to leave my wife, **God** told me to leave my job, **God** said to me that I am Elijah, etc. This is how all false religions and doctrines begin by having a **Spirit** of pride wanting to be special or more important than anyone else. It all goes back to the very root of sin, which is me-ism, I, I, I inflated to the utmost degree.

Okay readers, back to the story which I was sharing. So here I was, locked up in this motel room, thinking that I was sincerely seeking the face of **God** when pride motivated me. I was doing everything right. I was praying, fasting, reading my Bible, memorizing scriptures, and getting all pumped up. I knew the **VOICE** of **God** from decades of walking with Him, but pride had crept in unaware and began to cloud my judgment.

What I am sharing with you is pa**ram**ount because many famous men of **God** have gone astray even, ending up believing that they were Elijah or some other famous prophet. They heard a **VOICE** telling them something that was going to build up their egos, their self-worth. A lot of the affirmation people are giving and preaching today is simply nothing more than the pumping up of the flesh, which ultimately leads to destruction and death. Our identity does not come from who we are or what we accomplish but who **JESUS** is in me. "In **CHRIST**" realities! It frightens me to ponder upon how much pride still dwells in my heart and the hearts of other ministers because we can only take people where we are at. If I am egotistical, prideful, self-loving, self-serving, and self-centered, then that is the only place where I can lead people.

So, there I was, about the third day into this endeavor, when early in the afternoon, I hear a **VOICE** in my mind telling me, "There is a pencil behind the desk." In my mind, I saw an image of a long, standard, yellow school pencil with an orange eraser at the top. My did my heart ever gets excited thinking that **God** was going to begin to show me even simple little things.

Wow, would people ever be impressed once I came out of this motel room being able to tell them what was even in their pockets? Now, for me to get behind this desk, I was going to have to move this colossal television from off of it. The first thing that I did was move the chair out of the way; then I grabbed hold of this huge, monstrosity of a television; huffing and puffing, I moved it over to the bed, setting it down onto the mattress.

The desk was rather large, so I walked to the side of it and grabbed it the best that I could, picking it up on one end and dragging it slowly away from the wall far enough to where I could get behind it. Then, I very excitedly got down on my hands and knees and began to look for this yellow pencil with an orange eraser.

But something was wrong. There was no pencil there. Surely it had to be there because I know the **VOICE** of **God**; I heard it. It was there. It had to be. I kept looking and looking for a very long time. High and low I kept on looking for this pencil that I knew **God** had shown me was there. I had become obsessed with finding this very special pencil because this was the foundation upon which I was going to begin to have a worldwide ministry. All my success was built upon the fact that I must find that pencil.

All I can say is, thank **God** that I never did find that pencil!

Now, why would I say this? Because if I had found that pencil, it would not have been the **Spirit** of **God** speaking to me but a familiar **Spirit** speaking to and deceiving me. After this incident, I cried out to the Lord, asking Him why I could not find that pencil that He showed to me.

That's when the Lord began to speak to me very strongly, revealing to me my haughty and prideful heart. He opened my understanding to see that many men and women have been completely **HORN**swoggled, deceived, even hoodwinked by the devil through the **Spirit** of pride. You must always examine your heart considering scriptures, contrasting it to the nature of **JESUS** Himself to make sure that you are not operating in the wrong **Spirit**. I could share story after story of many women and men I have known whose hearts were filled with pride, arrogance, and haughtiness.

When this happens, they become extremely argumentative, self-centered, and self-loving. They cannot and will not receive correction, even when it's from the Word of **God** because their hearts have become so hardened through the deceitfulness of the love of self. More times than I can or want to share, I have met people who were listening to the wrong **Spirit**s and **VOICE**s. You could never convince them otherwise. Some of those people had only become delusional in their minds, always telling people what **God** has said, yet they displayed little evidence of **God**liness in their own lives.

Such individuals as these will continually justify the decisions which they have made even though they may be totally and entirely contrary to the **Divine** nature of **JESUS**, the life of **CHRIST,** or the Word of **God**. Others have had even more dangerous encounters with such deceiving **Spirit**s to the point of hearing **VOICE**s, having visions and dreaming dreams.

Such experiences are of the devil. Appealing to one's vanity and aiming to deceive, he can appear as an angel of light with revelation knowledge that is completely contrary to the Word of **God**. Every word, deed, thought, and action shall one day be judged by **God**'s Word, which is flawless. That is why we must continually judge our thoughts and our conduct per **God**'s standard so that we may be blameless and pure on That Day.

I am so glad that I had this ridiculous experience with the pencil because **God** continually brings it back to my mind to double check my motives and to make sure that the **VOICE** I am listening to is of the Lord. And still, even though I had this experience, I hate to admit that much of my **Christ**ianity has been me listening to the wrong **VOICE**s.

How can I say this? Because I look at what I have poured my life into, the results that it has produced and the fruit that has come from it. I am convinced that most people who say that they know **CHRIST** are listening to the wrong **VOICE**s because the fruit that is being produced is not bringing glory to **God**.

John 15:5 New American Standard Version "I am the vine, you are the branches; he who abides in Me and I in him, he bears much fruit, for apart from Me you can do nothing.

Receives a New Name

When this Ram's **HORN** is completed, it will receive a new name. It will now be **The TRUMPET of the Lord**, a **SHOFAR** that the priest will blow. The **SHOFAR** will be used to bring about the gathering of the saints, judgments, warnings, and the celebrations.

The **TRUMPET** was used by the tribe of Israel when they marched around Jericho. For seven days they had marched around Jericho not saying a word, but at the end of the seventh day, they blew the **TRUMPET**s. The walls of Jericho fell flat, and they defeated their enemy

They used to have seven **TRUMPET**s that would go before the Ark of the Covenant, which in the presence of the Lord throughout. The preaching, the roaring, the proclaiming of the Gospel, which is the **TRUMPET** of the Lord use to bring the people of **God** together. **God** never meant for Games and programs to bring his people together, but the preaching of the Word of **God**.

When I first was saved, I was not a music lover. I used to use music to edify myself in the **Spirit**, but I never saw the importance of it. But when I had that divine visitation of seeing the song of Heaven coming out of **God**'s mouth, my whole perspective was changed radically. Heaven is filled with music. Heaven is filled with amazing instruments, wind instruments.

Whether you know it or not, you are a wind instrument. Every time you open your mouth and talk, you prove you're a wind instrument. What kind of music is coming out of your mouth? Is it the music of the **Spirit**? Is it the music of **God**, or is it the music of the flesh?

As previously stated, there are probably over 93 million songs that have been written by the human race. More than 99 percent of the songs are nothing but flesh. There is no life, no power, no victory, and no transformation. All of these songs glorify the world, the flesh, or the devil. **God** wants to take his people and filled their mouth with a new song to the Lord. Almost every day of my life, I strive to sing a new song to the Lord out of the love and thankfulness that **God** has put in my heart for him.

Psalm 33:3 Sing unto him a new song; play skilfully with a loud noise.

Psalm 40:3 And he hath put a new song in my mouth, even praise unto our God: many shall see it, and fear, and shall trust in the Lord.

Psalm 96:1 O sing unto the Lord a new song: sing unto the Lord, all the earth.

Psalm 98:1 O sing unto the Lord a new song; for he hath done marvelous things: his right hand, and his holy arm, hath gotten him the victory.

Psalm 144:9 I will sing a new song unto thee, O God: upon a psaltery and an instrument of ten strings will I sing praises unto thee.

Psalm 149:1 Praise ye the Lord. Sing unto the Lord a new song, and his praise in the congregation of saints.

Isaiah 42:10 Sing unto the Lord a new song, and his praise from the end of the earth, ye that go down to the sea, and all that is therein; the isles, and the inhabitants thereof.

Now when the **HORN** is broken off, it is ugly, useless, and it stinks. I mean it stinks. Once they get the **HORN** off of the dead skull, then they turn the tip up towards heaven. It has a tip on it, which at one time was the most dangerous part of the **HORN**. This eventually gets cut off. Now, this tip is symbolic of the tongue.

James 3:1My brethren, be not many Masters, knowing that we shall receive the greater condemnation. 2 For in many things we offend all. If any man offends not in word, the same is a perfect man, and able also to bridle the whole body. 3 Behold, we put bits in the horses' mouths that they may obey us; and we turn about their whole body. 4 Behold also the ships, which though they be so great, and are driven of fierce winds, yet are they turned about with a very small helm, whithersoever the governor listeth.

5 Even so the tongue is a little member, and boasteth great things. Behold, how great a matter a little FIRE kindleth! 6 And the tongue is a FIRE, a world of iniquity: so is the tongue among our members, that it defileth the whole body, and setteth on FIRE the course of nature; and it is set on FIRE of hell. 7 For every kind of beasts, and of birds, and of serpents, and of things in the sea, is tamed, and hath been tamed of mankind: 8 but the tongue can no man tame; it is an unruly evil, full of deadly poison.

9 Therewith bless we God, even the Father; and therewith curse we men, which are made after the similitude of God. 10 Out of the same mouth proceedeth blessing and cursing. My brethren, these things ought not so to be. 11 Doth a fountain send forth at the same place sweet water and bitter? 12 Can the fig tree, my brethren, bear olive berries? Either a vine, figs? So can no fountain both yield salt water and fresh.

This fleshly, satanic tongue must be eventually cut off in order for the wind can blow through it for the craftsmen or the musician can blow an amazing **Tune** through it. This will be covered in the 10th step of turning a ram's **HORN** into a beautiful **SHOFAR**!

At this point, this ram's **HORN** is still filled with the cartridge, stinky flesh. They take a stick, and they begin to beat the **HORN**. From top to bottom they smack it all the way around. Smacking, knocking it so hard where you truly think that they are going to break this **HORN** in half. But this **HORN** is very strong. Remember, it was used to do battle with its enemies. They are tapping and tapping and tapping it with a vengeance when all of a sudden it just plops, falls out. It simply falls out. What falls out almost looks like a big old rotten tooth.

You might ask: Why is **God** letting me go through this terrible time? I feel like I'm being buffeted every which way I turn. I feel like I'm beat to death. I feel like I'm being abused. In these occasions, flesh that has not yet been crucified will rise up and say: nobody can abuse me like this. You can't talk to me that way. You can't treat me that way. This is the time we truly need to believe the Scripture that says:

Romans 8:28 And we know that all things work together for good to them that love God, to them who are the called according to his purpose.

Remember the apostle Paul talked about the much suffering he went through.

2 Corinthians 1:7 And our hope of you is stedfast, knowing, that as ye are partakers of the sufferings, so shall ye be also of the consolation. 8 For we would not, brethren, have you

ignorant of our trouble which came to us in Asia, that we were pressed out of measure, above strength, insomuch that we despaired even of life: 9, but we had the sentence of death in ourselves, that we should not trust in ourselves, but in God which raiseth the dead:

Now I looked throughout the internet. I could not find this teaching from anyone on the transformation of the ram's **HORN** into a **SHOFAR**. Now, the majority of the cartilage is knocked out, but the **wind of the Spirit** still cannot blow through it. It is still ugly. It still stinks, but a big chunk of the flesh is gone.

It's still twisted, and it's ugly, stinks. You still cannot see a glow in its exterior.

The Weeping Prophet

I was at a large gathering one night, which I believe was a Full Gospel Businessmen's gathering. I was 22 years old at the time. As we were worshiping **God**, the **Spirit** of the Lord was stirring in my heart. Tears began to roll down my face as I got lost in the Holy Ghost. I gave a Prophetic Word with tears in that meeting at Agape Camp Farm. Everyone acknowledged it was **God**!

Praising God at Midnight

I was working at Agape Camp farm, located in Shirleysburg,

Pennsylvania, in the summer of 1977. Every year they have a very large Christian gathering. One night, instead of going back to Belleville, I stayed at one of the worker's houses. They had three small children; I believe it was two boys and a little girl. We had a sweet time of fellowship as we all sat at the dinner table. I slept on their couch that night.

In the morning, I could tell that something was different about how the children were looking at me. At breakfast, the children just kept staring. I asked the **Father** and mother if there was something wrong. They told me something strange had happened last night. They were all sleeping when all of a sudden, they heard someone singing in a foreign language. It was so loud that they all had gotten up to see what was happening.

Supposedly they tip-toed down the stairs. They came down to see where the singing was coming from. They told me that they had discovered me with my eyes closed, and my hands were lifted up in the air singing in tongues. They could tell that I was not doing this in my own ability and that I was honestly and sincerely asleep! I can truly say I have no recollection of this happening.

..... God is a Spirit: and they that worship him must worship him in Spirit and in truth (John 4:23-24).

CHAPTER FIVE

THE MAKING OF THE SHOFAR

#5 The Grinding of the HORN

The **RAM**'s **HORN** in its present condition is ugly and utterly useless. It naturally has upon its exterior a dull variety of colors. There are also deep ridges, bumps, and nasty valleys. To turn this **RAM**'s **HORN** into a beautiful instrument, all of this must be eliminated. For this to be accomplished this **RAM**'s **HORN** must be taken to a heavy grinding wheel.

The **Craftsman** will begin to aggressively grind away all the ridges, the valleys, the bumps, and ugly pockets. This whole endeavor will entail a major renovation. There is a beauty that is in the **RAM**'s **HORN** that can only be revealed by and brought to the surface by grinding away all that is unpleasant, and by putting it through this radical process. I believe that this is very symbolic of what **God** must do in a believer's life to bring them into a place of usefulness.

When **God** takes you to the grinder, the sparks are flying. **God** grinds you, and he spins you at the same time. You will feel like your world is spinning out of control. **God**'s trying to grind off the ugliness, the nastiness, the meanness, but you still stink even after all of this.

Yes, you are being transformed, but it takes time. Moses went through this process for forty years. Joseph went through this valley of the shadow of death for many years. But the time came when he was ready. That is when **God** gave the Pharo the dream that would change everything.

Hebrews 12:7 If ye endure chastening, God dealeth with you as with sons; for what son is he whom the FATHER chasteneth not?8 But if ye be without chastisement, of which all are partakers, then are ye bastards, and not sons.9 Furthermore we have had FATHERs of our flesh which corrected us, and we gave them reverence: shall we not much rather be in subjection unto the FATHER of Spirits, and live?

Deuteronomy 8:5 Thou shalt also consider in thine heart, that, as a man chasteneth his son, so the Lord thy God chasteneth

thee.

Job 34: 31 Surely it is meet to be said unto God, I have borne chastisement, I will not offend any more:32 That which I see not teach thou me: if I have done iniquity, I will do no more.

Acts 14:22 Confirming the souls of the disciples, and exhorting them to continue in the faith, and that we must through much tribulation enter into the kingdom of God.

Paul gives us an amazing insight into this reality in his writings to Timothy!

2 Timothy 2:19 Nevertheless the foundation of God standeth sure, having this seal, The Lord knoweth them that are his. And, let every one that nameth the name of CHRIST depart from iniquity.20 But in a great house there are not only vessels of gold and of silver, but also of wood and of earth; and some to honour, and some to dishonour.21 If a man therefore purge himself from these, he shall be a vessel unto honour, sanctified, and meet for the Master's use, and prepared unto every good work.

It had been a weapon of war to the living animal and now it must be grinded, and grinded and grinded and grinded. This is **God** working on the outside of us and on the inside. **God** is working to change us inside and out.

Job 33:29 Lo, all these things worketh God oftentimes with man,

Philippians 2:13 For it is God which worketh in you both to will and to do of his good pleasure.

1 Thessalonians 2:13 For this cause also thank we God without ceasing, because, when ye received the word of God which ye heard of us, ye received it not as the word of men, but as it is in truth, the word of God, which effectually worketh also in you that believe.

Those who have swallowed the lies of the devil will say it does not matter what you do. It does not matter what you watch. It doesn't matter what you say. That's a lie. The devil is telling you that because he does not want you to become a Holy **TRUMPET**, **SHOFAR** for the Lord.

The wind of the **Spirit** will bring conviction. You know, they used to blow the **TRUMPET** to bring repentance. The Jewish people have a whole system in which they blow the **TRUMPET**. In the feast of **TRUMPET**s, it declared the need to repent. You need to weep, wail and cry.

James 4:4 Ye adulterers and adulteresses, know ye not that the friendship of the world is enmity with God? whosoever therefore will be a friend of the world is the enemy of God.

5 Do ye think that the scripture saith in vain, The Spirit that dwelleth in us lusteth to envy? 6 But he giveth more grace. Wherefore he saith, God resisteth the proud, but giveth grace unto the humble. 7 Submit yourselves therefore to God. Resist the devil, and he will flee from you.

8 Draw nigh to God, and he will draw nigh to you. Cleanse your hands, ye sinners; and purify your hearts, ye double minded. 9 Be afflicted, and mourn, and weep: let your laughter be turned to mourning, and your joy to heaviness. 10 Humble yourselves in the sight of the Lord, and he shall lift you up.

If we are out of **God**s, then will we need to fall on our face and repent. Now, today, people only want the **TRUMPET of celebration**, but remember the year of jubilee, they were to blow the **TRUMPET**, and it was a time of freedom.

Blow the TRUMPET. I believe that's what **Jesus** meant. The **Spirit** of the Lord is upon me because he's anointed me to blow the **TRUMPET** in Zion, to preach deliverance, healing and freedom and sight to the blind, and to bring liberty because it is the acceptable year of the Lord. That's the year of jubilee.

Up to this point, the **TRUMPET** is rough, ugly, and nasty. When they finally get a lot of the roughness ground down, it begins to look like something worth having.

This process of grinding away all that is ugly and nasty in our life can end up being a long process. This is due to the fact of our upbringing, and the evil that has been embedded into our flesh, through the transgression of Adam and our parents, environment! But **God** has begun a good work in us, and if we determine in our heart no matter what happens, we will keep pursuing **God**, ultimately **God**'s perfect plan will be worked out in our lives. Here is an experience that happened to me back in the mid-1980s because of the ugliness of pride.

My Neck Was in the Guillotine!

I had been pastoring in Gettysburg, Pennsylvania, for approximately three years. To be honest with you, if I had my preferences as to where to pastor, it would've never been here in Gettysburg. Even statistically, there are many places which are much more open to the things of **God** than this religious, stiff-necked, hard to deal with area. Gettysburg has come to be known as the ghost capital of America because of their ghost walks, **Spirit**ual séances, and for**Tune**-telling.

I am not talking about the **Holy** Ghost, either. Nor does this include all of the religious **Spirit**s that are in the area, evidenced by their cold, dead seminaries and religious colleges. I know that there are many who think that where they are laboring is extremely difficult. They may very well be right. For over 35 years, my family and I have labored in this field, seeing very little results, and yet when I go to other areas, **God** truly shows up. Please don't misunderstand me, yes we have had many moves of **God**, many healed, many signs and wonders, and yet seen very little enduring fruit.

People get healed, delivered, set free, and then leave to go to some lukewarm, seeker-friendly atmosphere. You might ask, "Why are you here, then?" Because this is where **God** has called us to labor in His vineyard.

Back to my story: So, I had been pastoring for about three years in this area, when one night I went to sleep as I normally did. This time; however, I had a very frightening and real dream. This dream was not just a figment of my imagination or some kind of stomach disorder caused by something disagreeable that I ate.

In this dream, I was confronted by one of the major ruling **Spirit**ual principalities and powers in this area. Here I was sleeping soundly, when suddenly in this dream, I was in a very large mansion. I could tell that it was a historical mansion built in the style of the late 1800s. I found myself in a very large dining room with fancy woodwork, chairs, and other furniture that one would expect in a very wealthy man's house.

I could tell that I was on the west side of the house looking towards the east when a young lady came walking through a set of very fancy, wooden, double doors. Right away, I could tell that there was something wrong with this picture and felt in my heart that I was in great danger, so I began to look around for a way of escape. Right behind me was a single, wooden door that exited the dining room. I immediately ran for this door, entering into a large kitchen with cooking equipment.

The floor of this room was made up of large white and black tiles with tables aligned from east to west in a long row used for food preparation. To my right was a sink with old-style faucets and other cooking equipment. To my left were cabinets, meat hooks, large cooking pots, and kitchen supplies.

What immediately caught my attention though was that right in front of me, approximately 20 feet away, was the most frighteningly tall and skinny man that I had ever seen. I knew in my heart right away that this was a ruling principality and power in this geographical area. He had on a three-piece suit, dark in color, with some kind of checkered shirt covered by a leather vest.

He was also wearing an old-style bow tie that was common in the 1800s. His face was long, ugly and skinny, yet highly educated and intelligent. Evil radiated from him almost like an invisible aroma that filled the air with a terrible, wicked stench. He was smiling at me with a very large, grotesque grin, almost like the Joker from the Batman genre.

Immediately fear, overwhelming fear filled my heart. I had just run from the dining room, escaping the dangerous young lady. Now, as I looked upon this evil **Spirit**, I completely forgot about the young lady in the other room. My instincts were to flee. I turned around to go back through the door I had just come through in order to escape this wicked, sophisticated, evil, and twisted demon.

As I ran back into the dining room, the young lady was still standing there, but now she had taken off her top blouse and was standing there with just a black bra on in a very enticing way. When I saw her, I was hit with a double dose of fear. Sweat began to bead upon my forehead, causing me to spin around and head back to the kitchen from which I came. Turning, I confronted the tall, skinny, sophisticated demon as he is coming through the kitchen door. He was laughing uncontrollably, looking directly at me. I was stuck right in the middle between this devil and the partly undressed demoness.

At that very moment, I woke up sitting up in my bed, shivering and shaking with fear and apprehension. This dream began to torment me for several months, not fully comprehending what it could mean until it finally dissipated into my unconsciousness. I never did tell my wife about this particular dream because it was so frightening and demonic. I did not want to tell anybody about it since I really didn't understand what it meant.

About five years had come and gone since I had had this frightening and terrible dream. In the interim, our new church building had been completed. Not only had we built a new church but a new parsonage as well, where my family and I were living. My wife and I had three sons and one daughter. Everything was so hectic in our house that it was necessary for us to find someone to stay with us to help with the children. My sister Deborah had been doing this, but she had moved away.

We took in an ordinary, young lady who attended our church to help with the children, laundry, and other family activities. Everything seemed to be going along just fine, but there was an undercurrent that began to slowly erode away our family unity. This young lady began to become a part of our family, laughing and joking, all of us kind of teasing one another. Unbeknownst to me, things began to happen slowly but surely like a frog being slow-boiled. I began to have wrong thoughts and desires creep into my mind. In the beginning, I cast them down, taking authority over them.

We had an above ground swimming pool in the backyard of our parsonage where my wife, this young lady, and my children would swim. We would all end up laughing together, splashing, and just acting silly. I began to find myself getting carried away with acting like an idiot. My wife noticed this and tried to talk to me about the fact that I was a little bit too friendly. Of course, I vehemently denied this, deceiving myself.

I was headed for a major downfall, and the devil was laughing all the way. It finally came to the point where something was about to happen that would destroy myself, my family, the church, and everything that **God** had blessed me with if **God** did not **Divine**ly intervene. The good news is that many times, the devil overplays his hand.

I went to bed one night as I normally did, falling into a very deep, deep sleep when, out of the blue, I was back in the very same dream from five years before, back in the very house where I had been previously. Once again, I was in the dining room with the same scenario. There was the young lady and the other demon laughing at me, over and over.

Once again in this dream, my heart filled with fear, my mind and my soul became overwhelmed with great dread when suddenly, I heard the **VOICE** of **God** speak to me from heaven: "This is that which you saw in the dream." Immediately, I knew in my heart what was going on in this dream. Up to this moment, I was utterly and completely ignorant of the trap that the devil had set for my destruction. My head was already in the guillotine with the blade ready to drop, and I did not even know it.

I woke up weeping and crying, broken in my heart over the lust that had begun to consume me. I woke up my wife crying and began to confess to her the dream that I previously had five years before. Then I told her what had been going on in my mind towards this young lady, confessing that my wife was right all along and that it was true that lust had become the focus of my heart. (Thank **God** nothing ever did happen). I wept, and I cried, then I repented.

My wife held me, and forgave me for everything. We prayed together, crying out to **JESUS** for help, thanking Him for His mercy and His grace. **God** had rescued me once again from my own **Spirit**ual blindness and fleshly lusts. Thank **God** for His mercy and the loving-kindness and forgiveness displayed to us by the Great Shepherd of the sheep, our Savior, and Messiah, **JESUS CHRIST**!

2 Timothy 2:25-26 in meekness instructing those that oppose themselves; if God peradventure will give them repentance to the acknowledging of the truth; [26] and that they may recover themselves out of the snare of the devil, who are taken captive by him at his will.

THE MAKING OF THE SHOFAR

Sterilization

At this stage the kosher HORNs are put in FIRE to sterilize them from any living creatures that might be left inside them. The HORN is an organic substance, so insects, worms and other pests can destroy it in time. (From the Internet)

#6 Placed into the FIRE

Once the **Craftsman** has painstakingly grounded away much of the roughness on the **RAM**'s **HORN**, he must now take out the twist and turns. If you look at a finished **SHOFAR** compared to its original condition, it will become obvious to you that the finished product is almost unrecognizable from the original. That is because the **RAM**'s **HORN**, in the beginning, was extremely twisted, distorted, and even flattened out in many areas.

How is it possible to remove such defects, twist, turns, and the flatness in the RAMS HORN?

Until I watched the process on YouTube, I would not have been able to answer these questions. The **Craftsman** literally must build a wood **FIRE**. We are not talking about a large **FIRE** but like a small camp**FIRE**. Once the wood itself has burned down, and there is a blue, red, orange steady hot flame, he will pick up the **HORN** with a set of tongs. He will then very carefully begin to move the **RAMS HORN** into the flames of this **FIRE**.

Back and forth, he will move the **HORN** over the flames, rotating it as he goes. It is not his purpose to burn the **HORN** or scorch it. This **FIRE** has an amazing effect upon the **HORN**. It begins to soften like wax that is on the edge of melting. The heat of the flames makes the **RAMS HORN** soft to the point where it can be changed, pliable.

FIRE!

From Genesis to Revelation, the Scriptures speak about **FIRE** over **500** times. The Bible declares that: **God Is a Consuming FIRE!** *Elijah called **FIRE** down from heaven. ***FIRE** was used in the consuming of the sacrifice. *A **FIRE** was constantly burning in the **Holy** of holies. *Chariot of **FIRE**, and horses of **FIRE**, and parted Elijah and Elisha asunder, and Elijah went up by a whirlwind into heaven.

Numbers 31:23 Everything that may abide the FIRE, ye shall make it go through the FIRE, and it shall be clean: nevertheless it shall be purified with the water of separation: and all that abideth not the FIRE ye shall make go through the water.

Daniel 7:9 I beheld till the thrones were cast down, and the Ancient of days did sit, whose garment was white as snow, and the hair of his head like the pure wool: his throne was like the fiery flame, and his wheels as burning FIRE.

Zechariah 13:9 And I will bring the third part through the

FIRE, and will refine them as silver is refined, and will try them as gold is tried: they shall call on my name, and I will hear them: I will say, It is my people: and they shall say, The Lord is my God.

God will cause us to be put through the **FIRE** of purification. I heard it once said: **when the FIRE comes, you will either harden like a piece of clay in the furnace or melt like wax in flames!** This is all dependent upon where your heart is. It is not the test that comes to us that makes us or breaks us, but our responses to it. **God** said:

Is not my word like as a FIRE? saith the Lord; and like a hammer that breaketh the rock in pieces?

The dead **RAM HORN** must now be placed into the flames of **FIRE**. Without the heat of the **FIRE,** it will not be able to be shaped and molded into the image that the **Craftsman** has in his heart. **God** wants to mold and shape us into HIS very likeness and image. Oh, how marvelous the mysteries of the kingdom are that are so far beyond our own natural understanding and thinking processes.

Revelation 3:15 I know thy works, that thou art neither cold nor hot: I would thou wert cold or hot.16 So then because thou art lukewarm, and neither cold nor hot, I will spue thee out of my mouth.17 Because thou sayest, I am rich, and increased with goods, and have need of nothing; and knowest not that thou art wretched, and miserable, and poor, and blind, and naked:

The School of hard knocks

As human beings, we are all subject to personal stupidity. Sheep are not very smart at all. I could do a whole book alone on the stupidity of sheep. At one time, we had a petting zoo. In this petting zoo, we had close to a dozen sheep. Sheep by nature are not smart. That is why **God** uses them as an illustration as an example of the believer. Sheep need a shepherd.

They need someone to lead them, guide them, protect them, provide for them, deliver them, and help them survive. **JESUS** boldly declared that he was the Shepherd of the sheep. **CHRIST JESUS** is the brains of the outfit. Throughout eternity, He and He alone will lead us and guide us. He is the Vine, and we are the dumb branches. (Do we realize that Adam and his wife were sheep before they ever transgressed and sinned against **God**? The man was created with the absolute need for a shepherd.)

Have you ever seen professionally trained sheep? Men have trained all kinds of animals: dogs, cats, elephants, bears, tigers, ..., etc. The list of animals that men have trained are endless but do you know one thing we have not seen? Sheep. Do you know why? Because sheep are known to be extremely stupid.

They are one of the only domesticated animals known in the world that cannot live in the wild. Dogs, cats, horses, pigs, birds; almost all domestic animals can live in the wild on their own. Why not sheep? Because sheep need a shepherd!

Now please, do not be offended by this statement. I am not demeaning you or myself. These are simply the facts. **JESUS** said that without him, we could do nothing. That anything that is worth speaking of. That is anything that the **FATHER** can truly take pleasure in. We desperately need **JESUS** in every aspect and dimension of our lives. Listen to what Scripture teaches us in the book of Psalms:

Psalm 119:71 It is good for me that I have been afflicted; that I might learn thy statutes. (Read this Scripture again)

Psalm 119:67 Before I was afflicted I went astray: but now have I kept thy word. (Did you hear what the psalmist said?)

Psalm 94:12 Blessed is the man whom thou chastenest, O Lord, and teachest him out of thy law;13 That thou mayest give him rest from the days of adversity until the pit be dug for the wicked. (This is a declaration of God working in us)

In the book of Hebrews, there is strong exhortation about how **God** works in His people using chastisement because of our stupidity.

1 Corinthians 11:32 But when we are judged, we are chastened of the Lord, that we should not be condemned with the world.

Pay attention because this next verse is such a bold declaration about what **God** is striving to do in his people.

Deuteronomy 8:3 And he humbled thee, and suffered thee to hunger, and fed thee with manna, which thou knewest not, neither did thy FATHERs know; that he might make thee know that man doth not live by bread only, but by every word that proceedeth out of the mouth of the Lord doth man live.

Many times, when bad things happen in our life, the enemy of our soul, the devil, and demonic powers are whispering in our ears that **God** does not love us. They make accusations that it is **God**'s fault that these bad things are happening. That the Lord is not faithful to His Word, nor to His promises. It is time for us to rise up, repent, speak the word, and come against the works of the devil. Yes, Lord, I admit that I am stupid without you and that I desperately need you more than anything in all of life or creation, "I Need You Because without You I Can Do Nothing Right!"

My Son was dying from rabies, & it was my fault!

When my son Daniel was 16 years old in 2000, he brought home a baby raccoon. He wanted to keep this raccoon as a pet. Immediately, people began to inform me that this was illegal. I further learned that to have a raccoon in Pennsylvania; one had to purchase one from someone who was licensed by the state to sell them. The reason for this was because of the high rate of rabies carried among them. But stubbornness arose up in my heart against what they were telling me, and I hardened my heart and did not listen to my conscience.

You see, I had a raccoon when I was a child. Her mother had been killed on the highway and left behind a litter of her little ones. I had taken one of the little ones and bottle-fed it, naming her Candy. I have a lot of fond memories of this raccoon, so when my son wanted this raccoon, against better judgment, the warnings of my conscience and against the law of the land, I said okay.

I did not realize that baby raccoons could have the rabies virus lying dormant in them for three months before it would manifest. I knew in my heart that I was wrong to permit him to keep this raccoon. But, like so many when we are out of the will of **God**, we justify ourselves. We are completely blind and ignorant of the price that we must pay because of our rebellion and disobedience.

Daniel named his little raccoon Rascal. And he was a rascal because he was constantly getting into everything. Several months went by, and one night, my son Daniel told me that he had a frightening dream. I should have known right at once that we needed to get rid of this raccoon. He said in his dream, Rascal grew up and became big like a bear and then attacked and devoured him.

Some time went by, and my son Daniel began to get sick, running a high fever. One morning, he came down telling me that something was majorly wrong with Rascal. He said that he was wobbling all over the place and was bumping into stuff. Immediately, the alarm bells went off. I asked him where his raccoon was. He informed me that Rascal was in his bedroom. Immediately I went upstairs to his room, opening his bedroom door. And their Rascal was acting extremely strange. He was bumping into everything and had spittle coming from his mouth.

Immediately, my heart was filled with great dread. I had grown up around wildlife and farm animals. I had run into animals with rabies before. No ifs, an, or buts, this raccoon had rabies. I immediately went to Danny, asking him if the raccoon had bitten him or if he had gotten any of Rascal's saliva in his wounds? He showed me his hands where he had cuts on them, informing me that he had been letting rascal lick these wounds. He had even allowed rascal to lick his mouth.

Daniel did not look well and was running a high-grade fever. He also informed me that he felt dizzy. I knew in my heart that we were in terrible trouble. I immediately called up the local forest ranger. They put me on the line with one of their personnel that had a lot of expertise in this area. When I informed him of what was going on, he asked me if I knew it was illegal to take in a wild raccoon. I told him I did know but that I had chosen to ignore the law.

He said that he would come immediately over to our house to

examine this raccoon and if necessary, to take it with him. I had placed Rascal in a cage making sure that I did not touch him. When the forest ranger arrived, I had the cage sitting in the driveway. He examined the raccoon without touching it.

You could tell that he was quite concerned about the condition of this raccoon. He looked at me with deep regret informing me that in his opinion with 30 years' wildlife service experience, this raccoon had rabies. He asked me if there was anyone who had been in contact with this raccoon with any symptoms of sickness. I informed him that for the last couple of days, my son Daniel had not feeling well. In fact, he was quite sick. When I told him the symptoms that Daniel was experiencing, it was obvious the ranger was shaken and quite upset.

He told me that anybody who had been in contact with this raccoon would have to receive shots. He went on to explain that from the description of what my son Daniel was going through and considering the length of his illness, it was too late for him!

He told me that he felt from his experience that there was no hope for my son. He fully believed that my son would die from rabies. He loaded the raccoon up in the back of his truck, leaving me standing in my driveway weeping. He said that he would get back to me as soon as they had the test results and that I should get ready for state officials to descend upon myself, my family, and our church.

I cannot express to you the hopelessness and despair that had struck my heart at that moment. Just earlier in the spring, our little girl Naomi had passed on to be with the Lord at 4 ½ years old. And now my second son Daniel was dying from rabies. Both situations could have been prevented.

Immediately, I gathered together my wife, my first son Michael, my third son Steven, and my daughter Stephanie. We all gathered around Daniel's bed and began to cry out to **God**. We wept, cried, and prayed crying out to **God**. I was repenting and asking **God** for mercy. Daniel, as he was lying on the bed running a high fever and almost delirious, informed me that he was barely able to hang on to consciousness. He knew in his heart, he said, that he was dying!

After everyone disbursed from his bed with great overwhelming sorrow, I went into our family room where we had a wood stove. I opened the wood stove, which still had a lot of cold ashes from the winter. Handful after handful of ashes I scooped out of the stove, pouring it over my head and saturating my body, with tears of repentance and sorrow running down my face. And then I lay in the ashes.

The ashes got into my eyes, mouth, and nose and my lungs, making me quite sick. But I did not care, all that mattered was that **God** would have mercy on us and spare my son and all our loved ones from the rabies virus. As I lay on the floor in the ashes, crying out to **God** with all I had within me, one could hear the house was filled with weeping, crying, and praying family members.

All night long, I wept and prayed, asking **God** to please have mercy on my stupidity. To remove the rabies virus not only from my son but from everyone else that had been in contact with this raccoon. I also asked **God** to remove the virus from Rascal as a sign that he had heard my prayers. I continued in this state of great agony for over 16 hours praying until early in the morning, when suddenly the light of heaven shined upon my soul. Great peace that passes understanding overwhelmed me. I got up with victory in my heart and soul.

I went upstairs to check on my son Daniel. When I walked into his bedroom, the presence of **God** was tangible. The fever had broken, and he was resting peacefully. Our whole house was filled with the tangible presence of **God**. From that minute forward, he was completely healed. A couple of days later, the state contacted me, informing me that, to their amazement, they could find nothing wrong with the raccoon. **God** had supernaturally removed the rabies virus not only from my son and those in contact with Rascal but from the raccoon itself. Thank **God** that the Lord's mercy endures forever!

Anointed to Flip Hamburgers

Kathleen and I were married On August 19, 1978. Three days after we were married, we headed to Broken Arrow, Oklahoma to attend Bible school together. When we got married, I did not have a penny to my name. She had to buy our wedding bands. Not only that, but she had lost her financial support, which came from her deceased **Father**'s social security.

Her **Father** had died when she was six years old in a terrible automobile accident, but the government stopped the payments to her when she got married. I, of course, had to pay off her existing college tuition. It took all the faith in the world for her to marry me and head off to Bible school with someone she barely knew, with no money or natural source of income.

When we arrived in Broken Arrow, Oklahoma, we ended up working at McDonald's. Our classes at the Bible school were completed by or before noon every day. That would give us enough time to go back to our apartment, change our clothes, and head off to work at McDonald's. For over three years, I had been pouring my life into the will of **God**. My whole heart's attitude was to give **Jesus** everything I was, I am, or ever will be.

Whenever I was hired to do a job, I determined in my heart to do it with all the ability that Christ had given me. I determined to have a thankful heart and to be the best worker that my employer had ever hired. My attitude was the same as I worked for McDonald's. Now my job was not very impressive, because all I did was clean tables, toilets, empty garbage, and do whatever needed to be done.

One day as my wife and I walked into McDonald's; I could tell that the manager was upset. I asked him what was wrong. He told me that his regular cooks had not come in for some reason. The customers were backing up with nobody to do the cooking. He said to me: Mike, you're going to have to be the chef today! I did not hesitate for a moment, but I told him that would be okay.

Now the story I'm about to tell you may seem incredible, but it is true! As I headed back to the grills, and the food preparation area, I cried out to **God** in my heart. I said to the Lord: **Father** in the name of **Jesus,** I thank you for giving me the ability to do this job. You're my strength and my wisdom. You're my hope and my righteousness. Now Lord, please supernaturally enable me to do this job for your glory.

As this prayer of desperation left my lips, I perceived the quickening of the **Holy Spirit** within my mind and my body. I had been watching to some extent what the cooks were doing as I was working at McDonald's, but I had not studied it in any detail when it came to the making of the sandwiches, the preparation of the food, or any of the other necessary skills that were involved. As I stepped behind the grills, divine knowledge began to flood my soul with what I needed to do.

The crowds were waiting out front for their food, and I was the only one there to prepare it. Why the manager himself did not step in to help, I do not know. Maybe he had never made a sandwich or prepared the food himself. I entered into another world at that moment where it seems like everything slowed down, but if you were watching me, it was the opposite, I had speeded up. In my mind, I saw exactly how to make the sandwiches, to do the French fries, to cook the food with no instructions and no teaching. I'm telling you I simply knew what to do by the Holy Ghost. And I began to do it!

I grabbed the different types of meat that need to be fried on the grill. I took hold of the fish fillets, putting them into the deep fat fryers. I very quickly put the frozen French fries into their baskets to be deep-fried. I began to move like a well-oiled machine, every step of the way, not making one wrong move. In the midst of all this action, I had complete, total, and utter peace. Actually I was quite enjoying myself moving in the quickening power of the Holy Ghost, making and preparing the food at McDonald's.

I'm telling you I was having the time of my life. I was literally lost in the Holy Ghost as I was running about in the kitchen. As I was moving under this divine quickening, I noticed the manager of the restaurant off to the side watching me. His mouth was hanging open, with his eyes bulging a little bit. He just stood there watching me running like a whirlwind preparing all the food. During that work shift, nobody came back to help me.

I just kept on putting everything together — the fish sandwiches with their tartar sauce, cheese, and lettuce. The French fries being prepared. The big Macs, quarter pounders, fish fillets and all the other necessary sandwiches being put together precisely the way they were supposed to. Believe me, as I tell you this story, I am not exaggerating one iota. My wife was there, and she saw it all.

All of the workers at McDonald's who were handling the

front registers saw me moving and flowing in the power of **God**. That whole day went by until my work shift was over. I just kept moving in the Holy Ghost, and that whole time, I never took a break, not even to go to the restroom. Not once did I get tired or weary. Not once had I faltered or missed in any regards.

It was completely supernatural. I was pumped up, energized, and quickened by the Holy Ghost. I have experienced this many times, especially when I have gone overseas and preached in foreign nations. When I use to go to England for 21 days, I would insist that brother Malcolm White would not give me any free time. I wanted to preach every moment of every day as much as possible to reach as many as I could. And dear brother Malcolm obliged me.

At the end of the day, when my work shift was done, the manager came to me. And this is what he said: Mike how long have you been a cook? He told me that he had never seen anything like that in his whole life. And that he was completely amazed by my performance. That is when I told him that I had never even flipped a hamburger.

I had never made one sandwich for any restaurant. He looked at me in utter disbelief. He asked me: well, how in the world did you do that then? I began to preach to him **Jesus** Christ, his supernatural life, and his divine ability that will work in the heart of any person who will trust and have faith in Him! I remember to this day his expression. He simply stared at me without saying a word.

It was the end of another glorious day, as my wonderful wife and I walked out to our truck to go home to our apartment. My heart was filled with excitement to see what **God** was going to do tomorrow. This is how I have lived my life for over 40 years.

CHAPTER SIX

THE MAKING OF THE SHOFAR

Straightening the SHOFAR

Now we reach the toughest phase – straightening the HORN. The HORN is very twisted and should be straightened. The Ashkenazi SHOFAR is straight at its beginning and twisted at the end, while the Sephardim prefer a straight HORN, pointing upwards.

Why do they prefer a straight HORN? We got an explanation from Zvika Bar-Sheshet, the SHOFAR maker: In the past, the Jews in Spain were not allowed to carry or use a SHOFAR, and it was necessary to smuggle it in the trousers. A straight shape made this possible.

Much effort is put in the straightening of the SHOFAR. Thus the Sephardic SHOFAR is more expensive (threefold). Tear and wear, which is massive anyways, is even greater here, and every second SHOFAR breaks when being straightened. (From the Internet)

#7 HORN Is Straightened

The **RAM HORN** up to this moment is still nothing but a **Stinky, Ugly, Still somewhat Rough, Useless, Twisted, piece of the animal cartridge!** As the **HORN** is held under the **FIRE**, it begins to soften like wax held high above the heat of the flames. The **Craftsman** by experience knows when he needs to remove this **HORN**, less it gets too much heat, or not enough.

As he removes the **HORN** from the heat, he puts one hand at each end of the **HORN**, placing the middle on his knee. Very painstakingly, and cautiously, he begins to untwist this deformed **RAMSHORN**. As he proceeds, he must continue to place the **HORN** back into the **FIRE** in order to keep it soft. From years of experience, he knows exactly what this particular **HORN** needs.

Every believer is dealt with a tender hand exactly designed for their own **Spirit**ual transformation and development by the Trinity.

Even as in Genesis when the said: **Genesis 1:26 And God said, Let us make man in our image, after our likeness: and let them have dominion over the fish of the sea, and over the fowl of the**

air, and over the cattle, and over all the earth, and over every creeping thing that creepeth upon the earth.

If you look at every man or woman of **God** who has cooperated with the **Holy Spirit**, the more surrendered and yielded, they are to the Lord, the greater responsibilities they are given. **Jesus** said that they who use the little bit they have would be given much responsibility.

Luke 19: 12 He said, therefore, A certain nobleman went into a far country to receive for himself a kingdom, and to return. 13 And he called his ten servants, and delivered them ten pounds, and said unto them, Occupy till I come. 14 But his citizens hated him, and sent a message after him, saying, We will not have this man to reign over us.

15 And it came to pass, that when he was returned, having received the kingdom, then he commanded these servants to be called unto him, to whom he had given the money, that he might know how much every man had gained by trading. 16 Then came the first, saying, Lord, thy pound hath gained ten pounds.

17 And he said unto him, Well, thou good servant: because thou hast been faithful in a very little, have thou authority over ten cities. 18 And the second came, saying, Lord, thy pound hath gained five pounds. 19 And he said likewise to him, Be thou also over five cities.

An amazing Revelation: One Day Is as a Thousand Years to God

Several weeks ago, as I was up early one Sunday morning preparing my heart to minister the message that I was to speak, the **Spirit** of **God** quickened a Scripture to me.

2 Peter 3:8 But, beloved, be not ignorant of this one thing, that one day is with the Lord as a thousand years, and a thousand years as one day.

For over 40 years, I had always focused on the fact that a thousand years to **God** is as one day to us. But this Sunday morning the **Spirit** of **God** quickened the first part to me. That one day with the Lord is as a thousand years! The revelation came flooding into my heart as the Lord revealed to me what this meant.

God is so interested in the US, that he literally has slowed up time in his realm where one of our days is as a thousand years to him. **What Exactly Does This Mean?** Let's for a moment, examine this. If you would take one of our typical 24 hour days, divide that up into 60 minutes per hour, divide that by 60 seconds in a minute, what would we come up with? A day would equal 86,400 seconds!

The next step is that we would have to take **1000** years, times **365** days, which comes up to **365,000** years. Times **24** four hours in a day, which comes up to **8,760,000** hours. Times **60** minutes per hour, which comes up to **525,600,000** minutes in one of **God**'s days. Now times this number by **60** seconds per minute! If my math is correct, this comes up to **31,536,000,000 seconds in every one of God's days**! Now, this number must be taken back into one of our typical days because remember **one day is as a thousand years to God.**

So, we must take **31,536,000,000 divided by 86,400 seconds in one of our days! This is how many minutes are in one of God's days.** Hang with me for a while longer, and you're going to see an amazing **Spirit**ual truth that will forever change your perspective on how **God** looks after us. So, if we divide **31,536,000,000 seconds** by **60** seconds, this equals = **525,600,000.** This is the number of minutes that there is in one day with **God**.

Then we must take **525,600,000** minutes and divide that by **60** minutes into an hour. This would come out to **8,760,000** hours in one day of the life of **God**. This means that our **24**-hour day to **God** comes out to **8,760,000** hours to **God**. This means that for every hour we live, **God** has spent **365,000** hours in that one hour watching over us. If we take this down to minutes, we would have to divide this number by **60,** which equals **6,083** hours for each minute. Which when you take it to the seconds it comes up to **60** hours per second.

Yes, each one of our seconds to **God** equals **60** hours. What is he doing in that **60**-hour period? He is counting every hair on our head. He's watching each breath that we take. He measures each heartbeat that we experience. Do not ever believe for a moment that **God** is not watching over you and me because he stands in the realm of eternity. When the **Spirit** of **God** quickened this to me, my whole perspective changed. What an amazing **God** we have to think that he would slow down time, causing every second that I live to equal 60 hours so that he could oversee every part of my existence!

THE MAKING OF THE SHOFAR

#8 HORN is put In the Mold

God puts you into his vice after the FIRE has come. It is while you are still soft and moldable. He put you under tremendous pressure before you lose your FIRE, passion, you're submitted and yielded heart.

A **Master Craftsman** has a wooden vice specifically designed for making **SHOFAR**s. The **FIRE** alone is not enough. He will use his hands and his knees to begin to straighten the twisted **HORN** as much as he can. But in order to make it as straight as possible, it will have to be put in into a vice. Once he puts it into the vice He tremendous pressure on this ram **HORN**. Pastor Mike, are you preach a message of works?

No, **God** has ordained me to good works, and I brag about **Jesus** because the good works in my life are not for me but **God**. But I guarantee that **God** puts tremendous pressure upon me in order to bring me to a place of usefulness.

Ask yourself how does a diamond get formed? They he say it's under extreme pressure. Now, you might say I don't want pressure. Well, you don't want Christianity then. I've got more pressure responsibilities) now than before I was born again. Before I was saved, I wanted to commit suicide over Mickey Mouse, silly little stupid stuff. Now what I have to deal with is a thousand times more serious.

Matthew 10:29 Are not two sparrows sold for a farthing? and one of them shall not fall on the ground without your FATHER.30 But the very hairs of your head are all numbered.31 Fear ye not therefore, ye are of more value than many sparrows.

Mark 8:35 For whosoever will save his life shall lose it; but whosoever shall lose his life for my sake and the gospel's, the same shall save it.36 For what shall it profit a man, if he shall gain the whole world, and lose his own soul?37 Or what shall a man give in exchange for his soul?

Romans 8:32 He that spared not his own Son, but delivered him up for us all, how shall he not with him also freely give us all things?

Jeremiah 31:3 The Lord hath appeared of old unto me, saying, Yea, I have loved thee with an everlasting love: therefore with lovingkindness have I drawn thee.

God is forever at work in us, bringing us to a place of usefulness in the kingdom. In order for him to transform us, removing all the twist, stink, ugliness, and uselessness of our lives will take time.

We must fully cooperate with **CHRIST**, **God** the **FATHER**, and the **Holy** Ghost in this process. Our hearts will have to be softened by the **FIRE** the conviction of His **Spirit** and His Word! He stands at the door of our heart gently knocking, wanting to enter in to a deeper relationship with him and us. In over 40 years of walking with **CHRIST**, he is still working on me.

Straight and Narrow Way

This Work of **God** upon our heart is described as a straight and narrow way that very few will enter in. Most of humanity will not want to go through this kind of pressure. Many will hang on to the wealth of this world, instead of letting loose to serve a better cause.

The rich young ruler was invited to become one of **God**'s anointed **SHOFAR**s. He seemed to meet all the criteria. Then the Lord said an amazing thing to this young man. Go sell all that you have, come and follow me, be my disciple, my **SHOFAR**. I will cause the **Spirit** of **God** to sing through you with his mighty wind a supernatural song that will bring deliverance and freedom to the multitudes. This is all you have to do, go sell all that you have, and give it to the poor.

This was too much for that young man. He walked away sad with his head hanging low. Then **Jesus** said to his disciples. It is easier for a camel to go through the eye of a needle, then for a rich man to enter into the kingdom of **God**. **Jesus** wanted this truth to be proclaimed to every believer. This is why it is spoken of in three of the Gospels.

Matthew 19:24 And again I say unto you, It is easier for a camel to go through the eye of a needle, than for a rich man to enter into the kingdom of God.

Mark 10:25 It is easier for a camel to go through the eye of a

needle, than for a rich man to enter into the kingdom of God.

Luke 18:25 For it is easier for a camel to go through a needle's eye, than for a rich man to enter into the kingdom of God.

If we do not deal with the love of the world, love of money and materialism that is naturally in our flesh, we will never be able to be used of **God** as one of his anointed **SHOFARs**. We are not talking about just being a believer. This is a high and holy place revealed to us in the old covenant. It was a prophetic word that Christ would bring to the human race.

High & Holy Way

We need to understand that what **God** is inviting us to partake of is one of the greatest offers any human being could ever receive. **God** has looked over all of humanity and chosen us to be instruments through which the wind of his **Spirit** can **THUNDER** forth. We dare not take this lightly.

Isaiah 35:8 And an highway shall be there, and a way, and it shall be called The way of holiness; the unclean shall not pass over it; but it shall be for those: the wayfaring men, though fools, shall not err therein.

Let us abandon everything for Christ, for he is worthy. Here is a true story of two young **God**ly men who sacrificed their lives in order to become the **SHOFARs** of **God**'s choosing.

MAY THE LAMB THAT WAS SLAIN RECEIVE THE REWARD OF HIS SUFFERINGS

Two young Moravians heard of an island in the West Indies where an atheist British owner had 2000 to 3000 slaves. And the owner had said, "No preacher, no clergyman, will ever stay on this island. If he's shipwrecked we'll keep him in a separate house until he has to leave, but he's never going to talk to any of us about **God**, I'm through with all that nonsense." Three thousand slaves from the jungles of Africa brought to an island in the Atlantic and there to live and die without hearing of Christ.

Several thousand black slaves toiled in the sugar cane fields under the burning sun. Three thousand slaves were doomed to live and die without hearing of Christ.

Two young Germans in their 20's from the Moravians sect heard about their plight. They [were willing to sell themselves] to the British planter for the standard price for a male slave [if necessary.]

The Moravian community from Herrenhut came to see the two lads off, who would never return again, having freely sold themselves into a lifetime of slavery. As a member of the slave community, they would witness as Christians to the love of **God**.

Family members were emotional, weeping. Was their extreme sacrifice wise? Was it necessary? The housings had been cast off and were curled up on the pier. As the ship slipped away with the tide and the gap widened, the young men linked arms, raised their hands and shouted across the spreading gap, "May the Lamb that was slain receive the reward of His suffering."

This became the call of Moravian missions. And this is our only reason for being...that the Lamb that was slain may receive the reward of His suffering! Amen.

These two men ministered for several years with some success. Both eventually came back and served the Moravian church as leaders. Their act, however, inspired a wave of Moravian missionaries that greatly impacted the world.]

CONSIDER JESUS

God says, I want you to be just like my son **Jesus**, and so he puts you into this vice of HIS WORD.

You could say that this VICE is composed of three elements.

#1 Jesus Christ

#2 The Word of God

#3 Pressure to Act upon these Two Realities

Jesus

Every believer being hears the **Voice** of **God**. They simply do not respond to Him. Some people have hardened their hearts to the **Voice** of **God** because of carnal flesh wars against the **Spirit**, and the **Spirit** against the flesh.

Before man committed sin, he responded instantly to the **Voice** of **God**. However, when man committed sin in the Garden of Eden, the seed of lust entered into the flesh and heart of man: the DNA of Satan. Adam and his wife partook of the forbidden fruit. Instead of running to **God** at the sound of His **Voice**, they found themselves running from Him. They became slaves to the dictates of the desires and lusts of the sin of their flesh.

Genesis 3:8 And they heard the Voice of the LORD God walking in the garden in the cool of the day: and Adam and his wife hid themselves from the presence of the LORD God amongst the trees of the garden.

The first thing you need to do is build a solid foundation to determine if what you are hearing is the **Voice** of **God**'s **Spirit** or the **Voice** of your flesh. There is the "**Voice** of the **Spirit**" and the "**Voice** of the flesh." You have to know which **Voice** is speaking to you. Granted, sometimes it can be challenging and a little bit difficult to determine which **Voice** is speaking to you.

The two main ways that **God** Molds His people is by looking and studying the LIFE of Christ and eating and drinking the WORD of **God**. You will need to read this chapter over and over: until you truly understand the two major ways that **God** molds us.

I will be referring to scriptures taken from the Book of Hebrews, and the Gospel of John. These scriptures will help you to build an amazing foundation for transformation. They will also help you to develop **Spirit**ual discernment for every situation. If you embrace what is revealed to you in these scriptures, your understanding will be greatly enlightened. Let us take a look at Hebrews 1:

Hebrews 1:1-3 God, who at sundry times and in divers

manners spake in time past unto the Fathers by the prophets, 2 Hath in these last days spoken unto us by his Son, whom he hath appointed heir of all things, by whom also he made the worlds; 3 Who being the brightness of his glory, and the express image of his person, and upholding all things by the word of his power, when he had by himself purged our sins, sat down on the right hand of the Majesty on high;

In Hebrews 1 it is revealed that in "time past" **God** had spoken to the **Fathers** by the prophets, but now He has spoken to us by His Son, **Jesus** Christ. According to **Ephesians 2:20 the Kingdom of God is "built upon the foundation of the apostles and prophets, Jesus Christ himself being the chief corner stone;"**

Please notice that in times past, **God** spoke specifically to the **Fathers** by the prophets. Now we have a more certain word of prophecy, a deeper revelation, a more precise understanding of the perfect will of our heavenly **Father**. Why? Because He is going to speak to us in a very clear and dramatic way. If we believe the words, life, and the example of **Jesus**, this will radically transform our lives forever.

Remember that all the words that had been spoken up to the coming of Christ were to prepare us for the coming of Christ. The life of **Jesus** is the perfect will of **God** manifested in the flesh. This is the mystery which had been hidden before the foundation of the world. Notice in Hebrews 1:2: "***Hath in these last days spoken unto us by his Son***." The foundation of my understanding of the **Voice** of **God**, the will of **God**, the purposes of **God**, the plan of **God**, the mission of **God**, and the mysteries of **God**, cannot be discovered in any greater revelation than that of the person of **Jesus** Christ! **There is no greater revelation of God's perfect divine will, or Voice, than what we discover in Jesus Christ.** I cannot emphasize this enough!

John 1:14 And the Word was made flesh, and dwelt among us, (and we beheld his glory, the glory as of the only begotten of the Father,) full of grace and truth.

If you do not understand that **God** is speaking to you very precisely through His Son, **Jesus** Christ, you will end up being mixed up, confused, and led astray. Learning to hear the **Voice** of **God** very precisely is only found in **Jesus** Christ: whom He has appointed Heir of all things, and by whom He made the worlds. Notice that Hebrews 1:3 boldly declares **Jesus** Christ is the brightness of the **Father**'s glory, the manifestation of the **Father**'s presence, and the express image of His personality. He is like a mirror reflecting the perfect image of the heavenly **Father** to all of humanity. **Jesus** declared:

John 14:9-10 Jesus saith unto him, Have I been so long time with you, and yet hast thou not known me, Philip? He that hath seen me hath seen the Father; and how sayest thou then, Show us the Father? 10 Believest thou not that I am in the Father, and the Father in me? The words that I speak unto you I speak not of myself: but the Father that dwelleth in me, he doeth the works.

Jesus Christ is the absolute perfect will of the **Father** revealed to you and me. The deepest revelation of the **Father** is only discovered in **Jesus** Christ. Paul, the apostle, commands us to have the mind of Christ:

Philippians 2:5-11 Let this mind be in you, which was also in Christ Jesus: 6 Who, being in the form of God, thought it not robbery to be equal with God: 7 But made himself of no reputation, and took upon him the form of a servant, and was made in the likeness of men: 8 And being found in fashion as a

man, he humbled himself, and became obedient unto death, even the death of the cross. 9 Wherefore God also hath highly exalted him, and given him a name which is above every name: 10 That at the name of Jesus every knee should bow, of things in heaven, and things in earth, and things under the earth; 11 And that every tongue should confess that Jesus Christ is Lord, to the glory of God the Father.

When we look at **Jesus** and hear His words, it is the **Father** we are looking at. The apostle, John, boldly declares in John 1:

John 1:1-3, In the beginning, was the Word, and the Word was with God, and the Word was God. 2 The same was in the beginning with God. 3 All things were made by him; and without him was not any thing made that was made.

All things were made by the Word. What "Word" is it talking about? The written word? Or Christ, the Word? It is obvious that it is the person, Christ **Jesus**, Emmanuel, **God** is with us!

John 1:14 And the Word was made flesh, and dwelt among us, (and we beheld his glory, the glory as of the only begotten of the Father,) full of grace and truth.

The reality is this: for us to rightly discern the Word of **God,** we have to know the person of Christ, discovered in the four gospels. What do I mean by this statement? When I gave my heart to **Jesus** Christ (on February 18, 1975, at about 3 p.m.), all I had available to me was a little military green Bible. The moment Christ came into my heart, I picked up that little Bible and began to devour it.

The four gospels of **Jesus** Christ: Matthew, Mark, Luke, and John, became my favorite books. I could not get enough of the wonderful reality of **Jesus**. As I read the gospels, I walked with Christ every step of the way. From His birth, through His childhood, His baptism by John (when He was thirty-years-old) where He was baptized by the Holy Ghost, and when He was led of the **Spirit** into the wilderness, tempted by the enemy; overcoming by boldly declaring: "It is written …"

My first three years as a believer were spent eating and drinking nothing but **Jesus** from the four gospels. Yes, I did read the Epistles, and they were wonderful; but nothing captured and captivated my heart as much as the life, the words and the ministry of **Jesus** Christ. I wept as I read of His sufferings, His crucifixion, and His death. I wept when I saw that the heavenly **Father** had to turn His face away from His Son, because of His love for us. I shouted at the triumphant conquest and victory that **Jesus** had over every satanic power.

Jesus Christ is the perfect reflection of the heavenly **Father**. There is no more perfect revelation of the will of the **Father** than **Jesus** Christ. I am extremely happy that I was not influenced by the modern-day church for the first three years of my salvation. When I eventually came to the Lower 48, after living and ministering in Alaska, I was shocked, and surprised, by what most Christians believed. I did not realize there was such a large variety of different interpretations of the scriptures in the churches.

Many of **God**'s people are extremely confused. Many ministers declare insane false doctrines that are so contrary to what I discovered in Christ. It is hard for me to believe that they even believe what they are teaching! They are being molded by distorted theology! To truly know the will of **God**, all you have to do is look at **Jesus** Christ: His words, His deeds, His actions and reactions; His lifestyle, His attitude, His mannerisms, His wonderful character, and the fruit of His life. I can truly say that since I was born again, there is only one person who I truly want to be like, and His name is **Jesus** Christ.

If the body of Christ would simply go back to the four gospels and walk with **Jesus** every step of the way: from His birth to His resurrection, to His ascension; much of their confusion would be gone. I believe that the primary reason why so many believers are being deceived by false doctrines and philosophies in America today is that they do not know, or understand, **Jesus** Christ.

Hebrews 13:8 Jesus Christ the same yesterday, and to day, and for ever.

In the Old Covenant, **God** says: "**I am the Lord, and I change not.**" Without truly seeing the **Father** through the Word and the life of **Jesus** Christ, you can easily be led astray by crafty men misusing scriptures. You have to see **Jesus** to understand the Old Testament and the Epistles of the New Testament. **Jesus** is the **Voice** of **God**, the absolute perfect will of the **Father**.

GODS WORD & BEING A DOER

The written word, the Bible, is the audible **Voice** of **God**. Because it is the **Voice** of **God**, it must become more real to you than anything else in this world. Believers tell me, all the time that **God** does not speak to them, but they are sadly mistaken. He speaks to us through The Holy Bible.

2 Timothy 3:16 All scripture is given by inspiration of God and is profitable for doctrine, for reproof, for correction, for instruction in righteousness:

The Second part of **God** Vice is the written word. Remember that **Jesus** Christ, His life, and His words, are the first major way that we hear the **Voice** of **God**; and this is the foundation that we must build upon for being shaped and formed into the image of **God**. It is only when this truth is established in our hearts, we can go to the written word, the Epistles, and the Old Testament, with understanding.

What must take priority - over all scripture - is what **Jesus** said and did. After this reality, we can go to the Epistles of Paul, Peter, Philip, James, the Book of Jude, and all of the WORD with divine and clear understanding. To illustrate this: some people are still teaching and promoting physical circumcision, Holy days, Feast days, Sabbath days, and New Moon days - because they do not know that **Jesus** Christ is the embodiment of all the Levitical laws. If you allow yourself to be placed into these man-made devices, you will always remain twisted. The process will never be completed for you to be an instrument in this world for **God**'s glory

Colossians 2:16-17 Let no man therefore judge you in meat, or in drink, or in respect of an holyday, or of the new moon, or of the sabbath days: 17 Which are a shadow of things to come; but the body is of Christ.

Many of the Old Testament miracles were types and shadows of **Jesus** Christ. The Passover lamb, manna from heaven, water from the rock, and the snake on the brazen pole. **Jesus** Christ is the will and **Voice** of **God** speaking loud and clear to the human race. Now, with this reality, the pure Word of **God** can work mightily within our lives.

Hebrews 4:12 For the word of God is quick, and powerful, and sharper than any twoedged sword, piercing even to the dividing asunder of soul and Spirit, and of the joints and marrow, and is a discerner of the thoughts and intents of the heart.

1 Peter 2:2 As newborn babes, desire the sincere milk of the word, that ye may grow thereby:

1 Peter 1:23 Being born again, not of corruptible seed, but of incorruptible, by the word of God, which liveth and abideth forever.

The very first foundation that we need to allow to mold and shape us and the one that will build an unmovable foundation in our hearts is **Jesus**: **the life of Jesus, the works of Jesus, the words of Jesus, the attitude of Jesus and the conduct of Jesus**. David declared that he hid the Word of **God** in his heart so that he would not sin against **God**. Furthermore, the apostle Paul shared this amazing revelation:

Romans 12:2 And be not conformed to this world: but be ye transformed by the renewing of your mind, that ye may prove what is that good, and acceptable, and perfect, will of God.

In John 17, **Jesus** is no longer speaking to His disciples. He is speaking directly to His heavenly **Father**. **Jesus** reveals some amazing realities and **Spirit**ual insights into how we are to become one with Him, the heavenly **Father**, and the Holy Ghost.

John 17:17, Sanctify them through thy truth: thy word is the truth.

John 17:19 And for their sakes I sanctify myself, that they also might be sanctified through the truth.

In the Book of Ephesians, the apostle Paul tells us that husbands are to love their wives as Christ loves the church. Christ gave Himself for the church: so that He might sanctify and cleanse it with the washing of water by the Word that He might present to Himself a glorious church without spot or wrinkle or any such thing.

Let me challenge you with a bold statement: Christ is the audible, visible, manifested **Voice** of the **Father** sent to the Earth in human flesh! All scriptures, from Genesis to Revelation, simply verify who **Jesus** is, what He accomplished, what He taught, and what He did. By looking at **Jesus,** you should never again be confused about who **God** is. **Jesus** answered all of those questions.

2 Timothy 3:16-17 All scripture is given by inspiration of God, and is profitable for doctrine, for reproof, for correction, for instruction in righteousness: 17 That the man of God may be perfect, throughly furnished unto all good works.

We have to look at the Word through the person of **Jesus** Christ. We will never really understand the Word of **God**, or the will of **God**, without looking at it through our Lord **Jesus** Christ. Many ministers are wrongly emphasizing finances, materialism, and other subjects because they do not know **Jesus** Christ, or what is important to Him and His **Father**! Ministers are constantly emphasizing the anointing when they should be emphasizing the reality of **Jesus** Christ.

Many are not even preaching and teaching about **Jesus** in the pulpit the way they should, because they are not looking at the

Word of **God** through Christ. He is the way, the truth, and the light. No man comes to the **Father** but by **Jesus** Christ. There is no other name under heaven, given among men, whereby we must be saved.

I understand the **Father** through **Jesus** Christ. I understand the Bible through **Jesus** Christ. Because of **Jesus** Christ, the Word of **God** is more real to me than my natural and physical circumstances. Let me share one of the amazing experiences I have had because of the revelation I have in Christ and His eternal Word.

HEALED Of a Broken Back

In the winter of 1977, I was working at the Belleville Feed and Grain Mill. My job was to pick up the corn, wheat, and oats, from the farmers and take it to the mill. It would be mixed and combined with other products for the livestock. One cold and snowy day, the owner of the feed mill told me to deliver a load of cattle feed to an Amish farm. It was an extremely bad winter that year. On arrival, I backed up the truck as far as I could to the Amish man's barn, without getting stuck.

The Amish never had their lanes plowed in those days (and they most likely still do not) I was parked approximately seventy-five-feet away from the barn, which meant I had to carry the bags at least seventy-five feet! I think there were approximately eighty bags of feed, and each bag weighed, on average, a hundred pounds.

During those years, I only weighed about one-hundred-and-thirty pounds myself! I would carry one bag on each shoulder and stumble and push my way through the heavy, deep snow to get up the steep incline into the barn. Then I would stack the bags in a dry location. As usual, nobody came out to help me. Many a time, when delivering things to the farms, the Amish would watch me work without lending a helping hand. During my third trip, something frightening happened to me while I was carrying two one-hundred-pound bags upon my shoulders. I felt the bones in my back snap - something drastic just happened! I fell to the ground at that moment, almost completely crippled. I could barely move.

I had been spending a lot of my time meditating in the Word of **God**. Every morning I would get up at 5 a.m. to study. I had one of those little bread baskets with memorization scriptures in it. I believe you can still buy them to this day, at Christian bookstores. Each morning, I would memorize three to five of them. It didn't take me very long, so all day I would be meditating on the verses.

So, back at the Amish farm, what I did next would determine my future. Okay, I could hear the **Voice** of my body, I could hear the **Voice** of my mind, and I could hear the **Voice** of my emotions. They all said: "You are in big trouble!" Instead, I chose to listen to the **Voice** of my **Jesus** and He said: **"By my stripes you are healed now!"** The **Voice** of **Jesus** is more real to me than my own body.

The minute I fell down, I immediately cried out to **Jesus** and asked Him to forgive me; for my pride, and for being so stupid in carrying two one-hundred-pound bags on my small frame. After I had asked Him to forgive me, I commanded my back to be healed in the name of **Jesus** Christ of Nazareth. Since I believed I was healed, I knew that I had to act immediately upon my faith. Please understand, I was full of tremendous pain, but I had declared that I was healed by the stripes of **Jesus**. The Word of **God** came out of my mouth as I tried to get up and then fell back down.

Even though the pain was more intense than I could ever express, I kept getting back up; then I would fall back down again. I fell down more times than I can remember. After some time, I was able to take a couple of steps; then I would fall again. The entire time I was saying: "In the name of **Jesus**, in the name of **Jesus**, in the name of **Jesus**." I was finally able to get to the truck. I said to myself: "If I believe I am healed, then I will unload this truck in the name of **Jesus**."

Of course, I did not have a cell phone in order to call for help, and the Amish did not own any phones on their property. Now, even if they had owned a phone, I would not have called for help. As far as I was concerned, I had already called upon my help, and His name is **Jesus** Christ. I knew in my heart that by the stripes of **Jesus,** I was healed. I continued to pull the feed bags off the back of the truck and let one fall on top of me. Then I would drag it a couple of feet, and then fall down.

Tears were running down my face as I spoke the Word of **God** over and over. By the time I was done with all of the bags, the sun had already gone down. I painstakingly pulled myself up into that big old 1600 Lodestar. It took everything within me to shift gears, push in the clutch and drive. I finally got back to the feed mill late in the evening. Everybody had left for home a long time ago, and the building was locked up. I struggled out of the Lodestar, and I stumbled and staggered over to my Ford pickup. I made it back to the converted chicken house and went back to my cold, unheated, plywood floor room. It took everything in me to get my clothes off. It was a very rough and long night.

The next morning, I woke up and was so stiff that I could not bend in the least: I was like a board. Of course, I was not going to miss work because by the stripes of **Jesus,** I was healed. To get out of bed, I had to literally roll off the bed and hit the floor. Once I hit the floor, it took everything for me to push myself back up into a sitting position.

The tears were rolling down my face as I put my clothes and shoes on, which in itself was a miracle. I did get to work on time, though every step was excruciatingly painful. Remember, I was only twenty-one-years-old at the time, but I knew what faith was, and I knew what it wasn't. I knew that I was healed no matter how it looked and by the stripes of **Jesus** Christ I was healed now.

When I got to work I did not tell my boss that I had been seriously hurt the day before. I walked into the office and tried to hide the pain. For some reason, he did not ask me what time I made it back to work. I did not tell him to change the timeclock for me, in order to be paid for all of the hours I was out on the job. The love of money is what causes a lot of people not to get healed.

They had me checked-out at the normal quitting time, and I left it. My boss gave me an order for feed that needed to be delivered to a local farmer. If you have ever been to a feed and grain mill, you will know that there is a large shoot where the feed comes out. After it has been mixed, you have to take your feed bag and hold it up until it is filled. It creates tremendous strain on your arms and your back, even if you are healthy. As I was filling the bag, it felt like I was going to pass out. I was in such tremendous pain.

I simply said: "In the name of **Jesus**, in the name of **Jesus**, in the name of **Jesus**" under my breath. The second bag was even more difficult than the first bag, but I kept on saying: "In the name of **Jesus**." I began on the third bag, and as I was speaking in the name of **Jesus**, the power of **God** hit my back. I was completely and totally healed: from the top of my head to the tips of my toes! I was healed as I went on my way. My place of employment never knew what had happened to me.

Matthew 11:12 And from the days of John the Baptist until now the kingdom of heaven suffereth violence, and the violent take it by force.

I have discovered the will of **God** through **Jesus** Christ and His Word. I am not letting go of **God**s will, no matter what anyone says or teaches. I KNOW the **Voice** of **God**: it is **Jesus** Christ. I also know that the second major way that **God** speaks to us is by Divine Scriptures.

Matthew 24:35 Heaven and earth shall pass away, but my words shall not pass away.

Proverbs 6:22 When thou goest, it shall lead thee; when thou sleepest, it shall keep thee; and when thou awakest, it shall talk with thee.

Luke 16:17 And it is easier for heaven and earth to pass, than one tittle of the law to fail.

When Transformation Happens

Transformation happens when your mind and heart comes into complete and total agreement with **God**, His Word, and His will. By the **Spirit** of **God** the apostle Paul said: "be not conformed to this world: but be ye transformed, (metamorphosis) or changed, by the renewing of your mind."

Romans 12:1-2 I BESEECH you therefore, brethren, by the mercies of God, that ye present your bodies a living sacrifice, holy, acceptable unto God, which is your reasonable service. 2 And be not conformed to this world: but be ye transformed by the renewing of your mind, that ye may prove what is that good, and acceptable, and perfect, will of God.

Amos 3:3: Can two walk together, except they be agreed?

Before your mind is transformed or renewed by the Word, you are like a caterpillar. The number of legs and feet that a caterpillar has varied. There is a type of caterpillar that has sixteen legs and sixteen feet; which they use to hold onto anything and everything they can get their little feet around. When that caterpillar becomes a butterfly, everything changes, including the number of feet and even the purpose of their feet.

All butterflies end up with SIX legs and feet. In some species, such as the Monarch, the front pair of legs remain tucked up under the body most of the time. Their legs become long and slender. Something amazing happens to their feet: within their feet are taste buds and whatever their feet touch they taste. It prevents them from eating anything that is not good for them. This could be the equivalent to discerning which **Voice**s are of **God**. As caterpillars, they were willing to eat anything their little feet took hold of. Now they become very picky and selective over what they eat.

You see, the butterfly (which came from the caterpillar) now lives in a completely different world! It is no longer bound by earthly things. It no longer has feet that cling to the earth. It is free to fly above all of the worries, fears, anxieties, enemies, and circumstances of life. It can literally see into the future and where it is going. It has overcome the law of gravitation by a superior law: the law of aerodynamics.

As believers, when we renew our minds and leave behind the laws of sin and death, we enter into a new world called: **The Law of the Spirit of Life in Christ Jesus!** We need to be very picky with what we eat mentally because whatever we place in our minds and in our hearts will determine what we are meditating upon. The scriptures say: "as a man thinketh in his heart, so is he …" (Proverbs 23:7). To know the will of **God** correctly, you need to renew your mind.

You and I cannot obey the **Voice** of **God** any clearer than that of the renewing of our minds. Everything that is contradictory to the Word, the will, and the divine nature of **Jesus** Christ must be dealt with. As we bring every thought captive to the obedience of Christ, our ability to hear **God** will cause us to soar like an eagle. Listen to what James, the brother of **Jesus**, said about the renewing of the mind:

James 1:21 Wherefore lay apart all filthiness and superfluity of naughtiness, and receive with meekness the engrafted word, which is able to save your souls.

What if I told you that your usefulness to **God** equals your level of knowing, hearing, and obeying the **Voice** of Christ? Of course, the obedience that I am referring to here is a true, divine faith. A faith that will take hold of **God** (like Jacob wrestling with the angel) and refuses to let go until there is a wonderful transformation in your heart and in your mind.

There are so many scriptures dealing with the renewing of the mind, and the meditation of the heart, that a whole book could easily be written on this subject. I will share a number of scriptures with you that are important to this particular chapter.

Joshua 1:8 This book of the law shall not depart out of thy mouth; but thou shalt meditate therein day and night, that thou mayest observe to do according to all that is written therein: for then thou shalt make thy way prosperous, and then thou shalt have good success.

Psalm 1:2 But his delight is in the law of the LORD; and in his law doth he meditate day and night.

Psalm 63:6 When I remember thee upon my bed, and meditate on thee in the night watches.

Psalm 119:148 Mine eyes prevent the night watches, that I might meditate in thy word.

Psalm 104:34 My meditation of him shall be sweet: I will be glad in the LORD.

Psalm 119:97 O how love I thy law! it is my meditation all the day.

Psalm 119:99 I have more understanding than all my teachers: for thy testimonies are my meditation.

1 Timothy 4:15 Meditate upon these things; give thyself wholly

to them; that thy profiting may appear to all.

Psalm 39:3 My heart was hot within me, while I was musing the FIRE burned: then Spake I with my tongue,

2 Samuel 23:2 The Spirit of the LORD spake by me, and his word was in my tongue.

CHAPTER SEVEN

THE MAKING OF THE SHOFAR

#9 HORN put under stream of cold water

The **HORN** is beginning to look good but is still not usable. If you stop here, it will be of no use to the musicians.

Now get a hold of this. Once **God** gets you into the vice, and he gets that vice tightened down, he plunges you into cold water.

Water baptism is symbolic of dying to the old and you coming forth into the new. Now the **Master Craftsman** puts the **HORN** which has been straightened in the wooden Vice to the extent that it can be, with it still being warm and pliable, He plunges this **HORN** which is still in its vice into a tub of cold water, or into a stream of flowing water.

The minute he puts it into the cold water, the **HORN** Solidifies. This Rams**HORN** is now placed into a position in which it will remain for the rest of its life. It will not go back to its old ugly, twisted, flattened condition.

Baptized in the Bering Sea

After I was born again, (1975) stationed on Adak, Alaska, I read within the Bible about water baptism. A person that after they give their hearts to Christ, they should be water baptized. This is symbolically declaring that you have died to the old life and that you have become alive to a new life. As I studied this scripture on water baptism, I discovered that they baptized in the name of the **Father**, the Son, and the Holy Ghost. They also baptized in the name of **Jesus**.

I went to a preacher that I had met on Adak and asked him if he would baptize me in the Bering Sea. Now, this is still in April. So we have a baptismal service where another young man and myself to go down to the Bering Sea. I have never experienced water so cold in all of my life.

Remember we're way out there on the Aleutian Islands, and

there were icebergs in the water. Not only was their icebergs in the water, but we were in an area where there were many killer whales, seals, and walruses.

The preacher took me out into the water, and as he put me under, I had him pray in the name of the **Father**, the Son, and the Holy Ghost in **Jesus**' name. I still remember as I came up out of the water. I was a 19-year-old kid, but I knew the presence of **God** had utterly engulfed me. I did not even feel the cold of the water or the air. All I knew is I had obeyed the scriptures and had been water baptized in the Bering Sea.

For a true believer, this is also an amazing example of what happens in our lives. I know as I went through this process, which many times are very slow and tedious, those things which I used to do, I do not do them anymore. The old Mike Yeager is gone. My buddies used to like Mike Yeager, but I was born again and filled the Holy Ghost, my life has never been the same. I fell in love with **God** and shared this with all of my old friends? They tried to kill me. But **God** protected me and did not let me die.

SONG: I WILL NEVER BE THE SAME

Lyrics

What a wonderful, wonderful change in my life has been wrought

Since **Jesus** came into my heart

I have light in my soul for which long I have sought
Since **Jesus** came in to my heart
Oh, oh, oh
Since **Jesus** came into my heart
Yeah, since **Jesus** came into my heart
Floods of joy over my soul like the sea billows roll
Since **Jesus** came into my heart
And there's a great change, great change
Great change in me
I am so happy Lord, and I'm so free
Since He brought me out of darkness
Hey, hey, into the marvelous light
And it's oh, oh, oh there's a great change in me
And I'll never be the same
No I'll never be the same
No I'll never be the same again, oh no
Since my life's been changed
I am not the same
And I'll never be the same again
And there's a great change, great change
Great change in me
I am so happy Lord, and I'm so free
Since He brought me out of darkness
Hey, hey, into the marvelous light
And it's oh, oh, oh there's a great change in me
And I'll never be the same
No I'll never be the same
No I'll never be the same again, oh no
Since my life's been changed
I am not the same
And I'll never be the same again
And there's a great change, great change
Great change in me
I am so happy Lord, and I'm so free

Since He brought me out of darkness
Hey, hey, into the marvelous light
And it's oh, oh, oh there's a great change in me
And it's oh, oh, oh there's a great change in me
And it's oh, oh, oh there's a great change in me
Oh, yeah!!!

Songwriters: Carol Cymbala / Carrie Gonzalo

Trying to Evangelize My Old Gang

When I got back to Wisconsin, immediately I began to visit my old friends, telling them about the wonderful Miracles **Jesus** had done for me. I not only went back to see them but also purposely attended some of their parties. I remember one party I was at and I was standing there off to the side, and I must've been smiling from ear to ear.

I was so full of the joy of the Lord; I could not help but smile. One of the guys walked up to me and offered me some alcohol. I turned him down. Somebody offered me some marijuana, some weed; I turned him down. Finally, someone said to me, well, Mike, you're not doing the alcohol, and you're not taking the drugs, we're offering you what is going on? And I told him, I said, I've got the best stuff in the world, and it's so wonderful. I don't need anything else.

The next thing I knew, I had a small crowd of people standing around me inquiring what I was talking about.

I told them about **Jesus** Christ, how he had rescued me as I was trying to commit suicide.

Now they knew that something had happened to me because my speech impediment was gone, and my hearing had been healed. The minute I began to preach **Jesus** to them, they stood there for a couple of moments, and then they scattered every which direction to get away from me. From that moment forward, nobody from my old gang wanted anything to do with me, even though I tried to continue to evangelize them.

Truskowski Tries to Stab Me to Death

After being born again for a while, I perceived in my heart that I needed to reach out and witness to the gang I used to run with right outside of Chicago. We were not a gang in the sense that we had a name or any entrance rituals that we had to go through. We were just a group of young men who were constantly involved in corruption, drinking, fighting, using drugs, stripping cars, and doing other things too horrible that I will not mention. One day, I was sitting in a car between the two instigators of most of our shenanigans, Gary and Claire. Both of these men were very large and quite muscular.

I had fervently shared Christ with them and the others to let them know how much **God** had changed me. They sat around drinking, using dope, and cussing while I shared the good news with them. I explained I was on a heavenly high that drugs and the world could never take them to. Most of them just stared at me, not knowing how to respond. They all had known the old Mike Yeager. The crazy and un**God**ly stuff that I had done. They had seen me many times, whacked out on drugs and alcohol. Now here I was a brand-new creation in Christ preaching **Jesus** with a deep and overwhelming zeal.

Now Gary, who was one of the main leaders, was different in many negative ways than the other guys. He was like a stick of dynamite, ready to explode at any moment. He had been up to the big house already and spent some time behind the bars of justice. He never did like me, but now there was an unspoken, seething hatred for me under the surface, which eventually exploded. We were coming out of Racine, Illinois, as Gary was driving the car we were in. Claire was sitting against the door on the right side in the front seat, with me in the middle. At that moment, I did not realize why they had put me in the middle, but it became very obvious.

Before I knew it, Gary reached up and grabbed a large knife from the dashboard of the car. I believe the vehicle was an old Impala that had the old-style steel dashboard. The heating and air conditioning were controlled by sliders in the dash. The knife had been shoved down into one of the slots. He pulled the knife out of the dashboard with his right hand, jabbed it high up into the air, and drove it down toward me very fast, trying to stab me in the gut with this knife. I saw him reach for the knife, and at that very moment, I entered into the realm of the **Spirit** when time seems to come to a standstill. This has happened to me on numerous occasions in such dangerous situations.

When I enter this realm, time slows down while my speed or movement seems to increase. You could argue whether I speed up or time slows down. I really can't say, though; it just happens.

The knife came down toward my guts in slow motion, and I saw my hands reaching up towards the knife and grabbing Gary's wrist to prevent him from stabbing me through the gut. I could not prevent the knife from coming down, but I was able to cause it to plunge into the seat instead. His thrust had been so powerful that the knife pierced all the way down through the Springfield car seat. He immediately pulled it out of the car seat and tried to stab me again. He continued to try to stab me as he was driving down the road. Every time he tried to stab me, I was able to divert the stab just fractions of an inch away from my privates and for my legs.

During this entire event, the peace of **God** was upon me in an overwhelming way. I was not shaking or breathing hard in the least; neither was my heart beating fast. It sounds unbelievable, I know, but it felt as if I were in heaven. The presence and the peace of **God** was upon me in a powerful supernatural way. I know this might sound extremely strange and weird, but I was actually kind of enjoying myself as I was watching **God** deliver me from this madman.

During this entire time, it was like a slow-motion review of a movie. Up and down the knife came as he kept on trying to kill me. This large muscular man was not able to kill a small 5'8" skinny guy. I just love how **God** does supernatural miracles. There was not one thing in my life in which I knew I was out of **God**'s will. I believe if I had been out of the will of **God,** most likely, Gary would've succeeded in murdering me. He kept on trying to kill me until up ahead of us a police car came out from a side road. Gary's car window was open, and when he saw the policeman, he threw the knife out the window.

Gary continued to drive down the road without ever saying a word about what had just happened. In this whole situation, Claire, who I had thought was a friend of mine, did not in any way try to help me. No one said a word as we drove down the road, but the peace of **God** was upon me like I have the invisible blanket.

Thou wilt keep him in perfect peace, whose mind is stayed on thee: because he trusteth in thee. Trust ye in the LORD forever: for in the LORD JEHOVAH is everlasting strength (Isaiah 26:3-4).

Truskowski Shoots Me with a Shotgun

About two days later I had to go to Gary's house. I really shouldn't have gone there, because there was just something satanic and evil about him. Just the day before, he tried to stab me to death! When I pulled up in my sister's red Maverick, he was sitting on his porch. When he saw me get out of the car, he grabbed a shotgun (I think it was a twelve gauge) which had been leaning against his house.

I walked toward him, and he aimed it right at my stomach. What was there about my gut that he was so enamored by it? There was no fear in my heart at the least. I just kept walking toward him. I was about twenty feet away from him when the barrel of the gun jerked slightly to the right as the gun went off.

The sound of the gun echoed through the valley. Nothing happened to me! As I think back to that day, I firmly believe an angel nudged that gun barrel with his little finger. If there was bird shot in the gun, no pellets hit me, and if there was a deer slug in it, I did not feel it go by.

It must have missed me by a matter of inches. I was not shaking or breathing hard in the least; neither was my heart beating fast. It sounds unbelievable, I know, but once again it felt as if I was in heaven. I walked up the steps of the porch and walked up to Gary. I took the gun out of his hand and leaned it back against the house. Gary just stared at me without saying a word. That was the last time I ever saw Gary. I have no idea what happened to him.

No weapon that is formed against thee shall prosper, and every tongue that shall rise against thee in judgment thou shalt condemn. This is the heritage of the servants of the LORD, and their righteousness is of me, saith the LORD (Isaiah 54:17).

What Does Water Symbolize?

Baptism symbolizes death to the old life. A new birth into a new life. Now Water and Resurrection are connected together hand in hand.

How Many Times is **"Water"** Mentioned in the Bible and How Significant Is It?

I you examine the references to water in the Scriptures scripture it will appear over 700 times. The first mention of water in scripture is found in Genesis 1:2 what's more, the last is found in Revelation 22:17. From Genesis to Revelation water streams directly through the pages of scripture. This reveals to us that there is a very important dynamic **Spirit**ual significance. Water is of extreme importance to all living things; in some organisms, up to 90% of their body weight comes from water. Up to 60% of the human adult body is composed of water. According to H.H. Mitchell, Journal of Biological Chemistry 158, the brain and heart are composed of 73% water, and the lungs are made up of about 83% water.

Water speaks of physical (or natural) conception

In Genesis 1:20

We read of the first mention of life, and this life originates from water, "…Let the waters yield inexhaustibly the moving animal that hath life…". This thought is again declared in the New Testament in John 3 when Nicodemus, a leader of the Jews, is making inquiries of **Jesus**. In verse 5, we read, "Except a man be conceived of water and of the **Spirit**, he cannot enter into the kingdom of **God**." Notice here, the water conception (physical) precedes the **Spirit** conception (profound).

We see the truth of this when a woman is in the midst of childbirth, and the child is going to be delivered. We have to wait for what we call 'the water breaks.' This water within the woman's womb encompasses the infant until birth.

Water speaks to us about God's Word

In Ephesians 5:26, concerning the bride of Christ, we read, **"That he may bless and rinse it with the washing of water by the saying."**

The Psalmist in Psalm 119:9 composes **"Fortitude should a young man rinse his direction? by taking notice thereto as indicated by thy word." Meditating upon the Bible has a purifying and fortifying effect on those who give themselves to the word.**

In the Tabernacle in the Old Testament, we read in Exodus

30:18 that Moses was to make a laver of metal and place water in it. This was to be arranged between the Tabernacle and the sacrificial stone. The clerics were to wash their hands and feet in this when they went into the Tabernacle "that they bite the dust or die not." They needed to be purified. The Lord was letting them know that they always expected to have their feet cleaned. We see a picture of this in John 13. The Lord **Jesus** washes the disciple's feet.

"Simon Peter saith unto him, Lord, not my feet just, additionally my hands and my head. **Jesus** saith to him, **He that is washed needeth not spare to wash his feet, yet is clean every whit: and ye are clean, yet not all."**

We notice what it says in **John 15:3 "Presently ye are clean through the saying which I have given to you."** In a believers life, we all need to be washed from the correctness of this world, we all need our feet cleaned.

Water identifies with us of the cleansing of the Christian. **God** gives to us prophetic words from the prophets of old.

Ezekiel 36:25At that point will I sprinkle clean water upon you, and ye might be clean: from all your griminess, and from all your Godlike objects, will I scrub you.

Hebrews 10:22 Give us a chance to draw close to **God** with a genuine heart in full affirmation of confidence, having our hearts sprinkled from an evil soul, and our bodies washed with unadulterated or pure water.

Water speaks to us of our Spiritual life

In Genesis 2, we read of the garden enclosure of Eden. It was watered by a waterway (v10). Without water, Eden would have become a desert, as plants, creatures, and people can't make live without water. This is a dynamic and **Spirit**ual picture of the life that Christ has provided for his people through the **Spirit** of **God**, and the word of **God**.

Exodus 17:6 Behold, I will remain before thee there upon the rock in Horeb; and thou shalt destroy the rock, and there might come water out of it, that the individuals may drink. What's more, Moses do as such in seeing the older folks of Israel.

Isaiah 12:2-3 See, God is my salvation; I will trust, and not be apprehensive: for the LORD JEHOVAH is my quality and my Tune; he likewise is turned into my salvation. Along these lines with happiness might ye draw water out of the wells of salvation.

Isaiah 55:1 HO, each one that thirsteth, come ye to the waters, and he that hath no cash; come ye, purchase, and eat; yea, come, purchase wine and milk without cash and without cost.

Jeremiah 2:13 For my kin or people have conferred two wrongs; they have neglected me the wellspring of living waters, and cut them out reservoirs, broken storages, that can hold no water.

John 4:14 Yet whosoever drinketh of the water that I might issue him should never thirst; however the water that I should issue him might be in him a well of water springing up into everlasting life.

John 7:38-39 He that believeth on me, as the scripture hath

said, out of his belly might stream streams of living water. (However this spake he of the Spirit, which they that accept on him ought to get: for the Holy Ghost was not yet given: in light of the fact that that Jesus was not yet celebrated.)

This water is the everlasting life that we appreciate now in Christ. That is the reason the scripture says in 1 John 5:12

"He that hath the Son hath life; and he that hath not the Son of God hath not life." Without water there cannot be life: Without the Lord Jesus Christ there cannot be unceasing life.

Revelation 21:1Furthermore, I saw another paradise and another earth: for the first paradise and the first earth were passed away; and there was no more ocean."

Revelation 22:1-2 Furthermore, he shewed me an immaculate waterway of water of life, totally obvious, undertaking out of the throne of God and of the Lamb. Amidst the road of it, and on either side of the stream, was there the tree of life, which uncovered twelve way of organic products, and yielded her natural product consistently: and the leaves of the tree were for the mending of the countries.

Revelation 21:17 Also, the Spirit and the bride say, Come. What's more, given him a chance to that heareth say, Come. Also, give him a chance to that is athirst come. Furthermore, whosoever will, give him a chance to take the water of life freely.

THE MAKING OF THE SHOFAR

#10 Tip of HORN Is Cut off

We mentioned this earlier in the book. So far, we have covered **nine major steps** that take place before the **SHOFAR** can be ready to fulfill its divine destiny. This tenth step has to deal with the **Tip Of The HORN.** This Tip is symbolic of our tongue, our mouth. Death and life are in the power of the tongue. Out of the abundance of the heart, the mouth speaketh.

James 1: 26 If any man among you seem to be religious, and bridleth, not his tongue, but deceiveth his own heart, this man's religion is vain.

The tongue can be our worst enemy or greatest weapon against the enemy. Our mouth was created to give praise and glory to **God**. Our tongue was created to do battle with the enemy. To bring every part of our being into cooperation with the King of Kings and Lord of lords. There are many scriptures dealing with the tongue.

Psalm 39:3 My heart was hot within me, while I was musing the FIRE burned: then spake I with my tongue,

Samuel 23:2 The Spirit of the Lord spake by me, and his word was in my tongue.

2 Timothy 1:7 For God hath not given us the Spirit of fear; but of power, and of love, and of a sound mind.

Acknowledging Every Good Work!

I cannot overemphasize the absolute complete necessity of dealing with your tongue. The tongue is the very instrument by which men speak in agreement with **God**, thereby being born again. It is our tongue that we use to release faith by speaking **God**'s word. It is the tongue that we use for battle in this fight of faith.

The apostle Paul said: I have fought a good fight, I have kept the faith! It will be a fight of faith for you to love **God**, follow **God**, obey **God**, serve **God**, surrender to **God**, and submit to **God** and to give Him everything. It is a good fight because a good fight is a fight that you win.

When you look at two men, who are fighting over who is going to be the next heavyweight boxing champion of the world, both of these men will be bloodied, bruised and beat up. Even the champion of this fight will be in this condition. Why do believers think that when you fight the fight of faith that everything is going to be just hunk-adore, peaches and cream, and cotton candy? Let us now look at another Scripture for this chapter.

Philemon 1:4 I thank my God, making mention of thee always in my prayers, 5 Hearing of thy love and faith, which thou hast toward the Lord Jesus, and toward all saints;6 That the communication of thy faith may become effectual by the acknowledging of every good thing which is in you in Christ Jesus.7 For we have great joy and consolation in thy love, because the bowels of the saints are refreshed by thee, brother.

The apostle Paul said that he had heard of their love and faith which they had in the Lord **Jesus** Christ. Then he says something quite amazing because he says that the communication or participation of their faith will become effectual by the acknowledging, sharing or declaring of every good thing which is in us because of Christ **Jesus**.

King James is probably one of the closest correct translations of this particular set of Scriptures. The apostle Paul said by the **Spirit** of **God** that the communication of our faith will cause our faith to grow by the speaking, declaring and acknowledging of every good thing which is in you in Christ **Jesus**.

The word acknowledgment means when you admit or declare something that is true and correct! So when somebody says something to you that is obvious, you acknowledge it with a rock-solid agreement. So when you agree with what **God** he has said about you, then your faith will begin to increase in your heart. Let me give you some simple biblical examples.

1 John 4:4 Ye are of God, little children, and have overcome them: because greater is he that is in you, than he that is in the world.

1 John 5:4 For whatsoever is born of God overcometh the world: and this is the victory that overcometh the world, even our faith.

Romans 8:31 What shall we then say to these things? If God be for us, who can be against us?

Romans 8:37 Nay, in all these things we are more than conquerors through him that loved us.

Hebrews 13:5 Let your conversation be without covetousness; and be content with such things as ye have: for he hath said, I will never leave thee, nor forsake thee.

Philippians 4:13 I can do all things through Christ, which strengtheneth me.

When you begin to agree verbally, out loud with what **God** has declared about you in his word, it will bring faith. This is also the process by which you cut off the tip of the **HORN**. Now, the word communication means to participate, to partake of, and to become one with. There are certain things that **God** declares about you and me that is absolute truth.

Then there are divine truths that **God** wants you and I to become, but we are not there yet. There are many examples that I could use, but let me use one in particular. Many so-called believers are declaring they are righteous in Christ by faith, but yet they are living like the devil. They think that faith is just a confession when it actually must be apprehended and worked out by faith in Christ **Jesus**. Another example is that **God** declares:

1 Peter 1:15 But as he which hath called you is holy, so be ye holy in all manner of conversation;16 Because it is written, Be ye holy; for I am holy.

You can declare you're holy all you want, but until it is manifested in your heart and your life, you are deceiving nobody but yourself. That's where the Scripture would apply in the book of James 1:22

James 1:22 But be ye doers of the word, and not hearers only, deceiving your own selves.23 For if any be a hearer of the

word, and not a doer, he is like unto a man beholding his natural face in a glass:24 For he beholdeth himself, and goeth his way, and straightway forgetteth what manner of man he was.25 But whoso looketh into the perfect law of liberty, and continueth therein, he being not a forgetful hearer, but a doer of the work, this man shall be blessed in his deed.

Did you notice in verse 25 it says a doer of the work? In Philippians, it says that we must work out our salvation with fear and trembling. Now we know Christ lives in us by faith, and people love to make good confessions about themselves, which is wonderful, but there is a difference between telling the truth and lying to yourself.

You can walk around and declare you're full of the fruit of the **Spirit** all day long when there's no truth to it. What are the nine fruits of the **Spirit** in Galatians 5? Love, joy, peace, long-suffering, gentleness, goodness, faith, meekness, and self-control. You can claim that these are operating in your life when they are not.

We need a **Spirit** of discernment when it comes to the declaring what is true in us now, and those things which we still need to work out. For over 40 years, I've heard a lot of phony baloney, hot air teaching because people are not rightly discerning the word of truth. If you are telling people that you are righteous, then they better see the evidence of that righteousness. Yes, the Scripture does declare that we are made righteous through **Jesus** Christ, but it is because of his divine nature and his word at work in us, as we are being doers of the word.

2 Corinthians 5:21 For he hath made him to be sin for us, who knew no sin; that we might be made the righteousness of God in him.

Romans 6:18Being then made free from sin, ye became the servants of righteousness.

Romans 6:22 But now being made free from sin, and become servants to God, ye have your fruit unto holiness, and the end everlasting life.

Jesus made an amazing statement in the gospel of John.

John 1:12 But as many as received him, to them gave he power to become the sons of God, even to them that believe on his name:

Did you notice **Jesus** said to become, how do we do that? We must do it with the faith that produces action and obedience that we have been ordained to walk in. We are dealing here with two different issues.

#1 The Acknowledgment of every good thing that is in us by Christ Jesus!

#2 The divine elements which God desires to be manifested and matured in us!

You can proclaim all you want you are full of faith, but that does not make it so. Now we can say **God** will never leave us nor forsake us, or greater is he that is in me then he that's in the world, or **God** supplies all of my needs according to his riches in glory, or if **God** before me who can be against me.

Proclaiming that you're righteous in **Jesus** Christ even when you are committing adultery, stealing, lying, cheating being ugly and nasty in your attitude and character is nothing but a lie. That is not faith, but it is the **Spirit** of deception at work in you.

The communication of your faith is when you acknowledge every good thing, every good thing that Christ has accomplished for you. I knowledge by his stripes I am healed! I say to myself by his stripes I am healed. And I then begin to thank him and praise him for it even though I do not feel it or see it. Your brain is always working; you're always thinking, most likely muttering to yourself. And what is it that you are thinking and speaking? We need to think and speak that which Christ has accomplished for us.

The tip of the old man, the tongue, the **HORN** will be cut off by the acknowledging of every good thing that **God** has done for you through **Jesus** Christ. When these truths get deep into your heart, there will be a change in what comes out of your mouth. It will be automatic and spontaneous. This is where we need to live.

Jesus said rejoice because your names are written down in heaven, so Lord I rejoiced that my name is written in heaven. You and I have never seen our name in heaven, but **Jesus** said it so I knowledge it. I acknowledge I am, I have, and can do what **God** says I am, can do, and have to myself. It's not as some would teach you that you have to tell everybody these truths about yourself. You have to speak them to yourself in faith. Here is a wonderful revealing of this truth discovered in the book of Jeremiah.

Jeremiah 1:4 Then the word of the LORD came unto me, saying,5 Before I formed thee in the belly I knew thee, and before thou camest forth out of the womb I sanctified thee, and I ordained thee a prophet unto the nations.6 Then said I, Ah, Lord GOD! behold, I cannot speak: for I am a child.

7 But the LORD said unto me, Say not, I am a child: for thou shalt go to all that I shall send thee, and whatsoever I

command thee thou shalt speak.8 Be not afraid of their faces: for I am with thee to deliver thee, saith the LORD.9 Then the LORD put forth his hand, and touched my mouth. And the LORD said unto me, Behold, I have put my words in thy mouth.10 See, I have this day set thee over the nations and over the kingdoms, to root out, and to pull down, and to destroy, and to throw down, to build, and to plant.

God had a wonderful plan for Jeremiah. I believe that **God** has a plan for every person that was ever born, but most do not believe or accept it. **"many are called; few are chosen. "**

God said that he would have all men to repent and to come to the knowledge of the truth, and yet people do not embrace **God**'s plan for their lives! This is the difference between sheep and goats. Most of what they call Christianity today is nothing but little clicks and clubs where people are just trying to impress one another.

After this experience that Jeremiah had with **God,** his life was never the same. From that moment forward, he never argued with what the Lord had spoken to him. Jeremiah said exactly what he had heard **God** say to him: I am a prophet, and I am sent to the nations in order to warn them of coming judgment. He had to be saying this to himself in order two cut of the tip of the old **HORN**, and for faith to continue to operate in his life to fulfill this difficult task that the Lord had given to him. If you and I are going to fulfill the will of **God** for our lives, we are going to have to begin to talk to ourselves in the same way. You need to declare in the name of **Jesus** Christ: I will love **God**, I will serve **God**, I will follow **God**, and I will go all the way for **Jesus** because greater is he that is in me then he that is in the world.

Another example is when and Angel came to Mary, the mother of Christ, and said blessed art thou among women. **God** has chosen you to be the mother of the Savior of the world. The Holy Ghost will come upon you. Therefore that which you conceive will be of the **Holy Spirit,** and you will give birth to the son of **God**, even though you have never known a man. She said, to let it be done to me even according to your word.

Luke 1:38 And Mary said, Behold the handmaid of the Lord; be it unto me according to thy word. And the angel departed from her.

Faith will come as you acknowledge and declare what **God** has said about you and for you to yourself.

Whatever you do, do not repeat what fleshly people say about you! They are not the foundation that you build your life upon. Praise **God;** we build our life upon **Jesus** Christ and him alone. When you hear the **Voice** of **God** {there needs to be evidence in your life that you hear his **Voice**} you need to immediately say what he says about you, what you're going to do, and where you're going, and act upon it!

God Has Not Given Us a Spirit of Fear

There is no fear of what men will do to you, or of sickness, or disease, or poverty, or financial lack, or plagues, or afflictions. There is no fear, there is no worry, and there is no torment when we are walking in the realm of faith. You will have peace that passes all understanding, joy unspeakable, and full of glory. When somebody is sick in the natural, we can put our hands on their forehead and see if they are running a fever.

The doctor can have you open your mouth, and he will look at the tonsils or your tongue. Symptoms in your physical body will reveal your sickness by certain manifestations. This is also true when it comes to divine faith. If you are truly operating in faith than the divine attributes of Christ will be manifested. The nine fruits of the **Spirit** will be evident. You will be living a holy separated and consecrated life for **God**. If you are not, then it is evidence that you need to step back into that realm of faith.

1 John 5:4 For whatsoever is born of God overcometh the world: and this is the victory that overcometh the world, even our faith.

Praying in the Holy Ghost!

We are looking at the 20th Way in which faith will come. This truth can be discovered in the book of Jude verse 20.

Jude 20 But ye, beloved, building up yourselves on your most holy faith, praying in the Holy Ghost,

If you will study this Scripture in other translations, it declares that we must fortify, strengthen, and establish our most holy faith! How do we do this? By praying in the Holy Ghost. I do not believe this is only speaking about praying in the gift of tongues which you received when you received the baptism in the Holy Ghost, but it is also speaking about the Holy Ghost leading you in your prayer time. The **Spirit** of the Lord himself will put the words in your mouth that need to be spoken.

2 Samuel 23:2 The Spirit of the Lord spake by me, and his word was in my tongue. Psalm 45: the 1......my tongue is the pen of a ready writer.

When you build yourself up in your most holy faith, this **Spirit**ual response is that it will take hold of the holiness of **God**, it takes hold of the will of **God**, and it takes hold of the character and the divine nature of **God**. There is a teaching that I have done, which reveals 10 biblical benefits that take place when you pray in tongues!

Out of the ten gifts of the Holy Ghost revealed within the Scriptures, tongues is one of the simplest that Christ has given to the church. This tongues that I'm referring to is not the same diversity tongues that need to be interpreted. It is your own personal prayer language that the Holy Ghost will give you to communicate to **God**.

Romans 8:26 Likewise the Spirit also helpeth our infirmities: for we know not what we should pray for as we ought: but the Spirit itself maketh intercession for us with groanings which cannot be uttered.

The exercising of this **God**-given language opens the door wide for the manifestation of the other nine gifts of the **Spirit**. It takes faith to believe that **God** is speaking through you in this supernatural language, which sometimes sounds like baby talk. I asked the Lord one time why he would give his people a language that sounded ridiculous? He spoke to my heart and said, I do it to humble my people. You must be as a child to enter into the kingdom of heaven.

Ephesians 6:18 Praying always with all prayer and

supplication in the Spirit,

Let me share an amazing story about how I was baptized in the Holy Ghost and the difference it made in my life.

How God Supernaturally Healed Me of Being Tongue-Tied!

After I gave my heart to Christ, a divine hunger and thirst for the Word of **God** began to possess me. I practically devoured Matthew, Mark, Luke, and John. **Jesus** became my hero in every sense of the word in every area of my thoughts and daily living. He became my sole reason for getting up every day and going to work, eating, sleeping, and living. I discovered that everything I did was based on a desire of wanting to please Him.

One day I was reading my Bible and discovered where **Jesus** said that it was necessary for him to leave. That because when he would go back to the **Father**, he would send the promise of the Holy Ghost to make us a witness. Furthermore, I learned it was His will for me to be filled to overflowing with the Holy Ghost and that the Holy Ghost would empower and equip me to be a witness an ambassador for **God**. The Holy Ghost would also lead me and guide me into all truth.

With all of my heart, I desperately wanted to reach the lost for **Jesus** Christ in order for they could also experience the same love and freedom that I was now walking in. I searched the Scriptures to confirm this experience. In the book of Joel, in the old covenant, the four Gospels and especially in the book of acts, I discovered the will of **God** when it comes to this baptism. I perceived in my heart that I needed to receive this baptism the same way that I had received salvation.

I had to look to Christ and trust by faith that he would give to me this baptism of the **Spirit**. It declared in the book of acts that after they were baptized in the Holy Ghost, they all began to speak in a heavenly language. I had not been around what we would call Pentecostal people, so I had never heard anybody else speak in this heavenly language, but that did not really matter to me, because it was within the Scriptures.

Acts 2:39 For the promise is unto you, and to your children, and to all that are afar off, even as many as the Lord our God shall call.

I remember getting on my knees next to my bunk bed where I cried out and asked **God** to fill me with the Holy Ghost so I could be a witness. As I was crying out to **God,** something began to happen on the inside of me. It felt like hot buckets of oil was beginning to be poured into me. Something then began to rise up out of my innermost being. Before I knew what I was doing, a new language came bubbling out of my mouth, which I had never heard before or been taught to speak. I began to speak in a heavenly tongue.

Now up to this time, I had a terrible speech impediment. You see, I had been born tongue-tied. Yes, they had operated on me, and I had gone to speech therapy, and yet most people could not understand what I was saying. I could not even pronounce my own last name YEAGER properly. My tongue simply refused to move in a way in which I could pronounce my Rs.

After I was done praying in this new language, I discovered to my absolute surprise that my speech impediment was instantly and completely gone! From that time on, I have never stopped preaching **Jesus** Christ. For almost 40 years, I have proclaimed the truth of **Jesus** Christ to as many as I can.

For the First Time, She Could Understand Me

About four months after I gave my heart to Christ, I went back to my hometown, Mukwonago, Wisconsin; I immediately went to see one of my best friends to share with him my conversion experience. It was his sister I had been dating for the last three years. I wrote her a letter telling her what happened to me, and how **God** had gloriously set me free from drugs, alcohol, and all of my worldly living. This caused her to cut me off completely as if I had lost my mind. Praise **God**! I had lost my mind by receiving the mind of Christ. My friend's mother was listening while I was speaking to her son, and out of nowhere, she said, "Mike, what happened to you?" I told her how I had been delivered from drugs and immorality because I gave my heart to **Jesus**. She said, "No, that's not what I'm talking about. After many years of knowing you, this is the 1st time I can fully understand what you are saying."

You see, my speech was so garbled that it was very difficult for people to truly understand exactly what I was saying. Those who know me now would not have recognized the old me. Before I was baptized in the Holy Ghost, you would not have been able to understand most of I said. I'm still trying to make up for the 1st nineteen years when I could not speak properly.

Victory over Tumors

I woke up one morning with tremendous pain in my lower abdomen. I lifted up my shirt and looked down where the pain was. There was a lump on my abdomen about the size of an acorn. I laid my hands on it immediately, commanding it to go.

I said, "You lying devil, by the stripes of **Jesus** I am healed and made whole." After I spoke to the lump, the pain became excruciating and overwhelmingly worse. All that day, I walked the floor crying out to **God** and praising him that His Word is real and true.

I went for a walk on the mountain right behind the parsonage. It was a long day before I got to sleep that night. When I awoke the next morning, the pain was even more severe. It felt like somebody was stabbing me in my gut with a knife. I lifted up my shirt and looked, and there was another lump. Now I had two lumps in my lower abdomen.

I laid my hands on them, commanding them to go. Tears were rolling down my face as I spoke the Word. I lifted my hands toward heaven and kept praising **God** that I was healed. Even though I did not see any change, I kept praising **God**. All the symptoms were telling me that **God**'s Word is a lie and that I was not healed by the stripes of **Jesus**. But I knew that I was healed. It was another long day. It seemed as if I could never get to sleep that night. The pain was continual and non-stop!

When I got up the next morning, the pain had intensified even more. Once again, I looked at my abdomen, and to my shock, there was another lump the size of an acorn. Now I had three of these nasty lumps, and each was about the size of an acorn. I did not think that the pain could get any worse, but it was. Once again, I laid my hands on these tumors, commanding them to go in the name of **Jesus** Christ of Nazareth.

I declared that by the stripes of **Jesus,** I am healed! It felt like a knife sticking in my gut all that day and night. I lifted my hands, and with tears rolling down my face, kept praising **God** that I was healed.

By faith, I began to dance before the Lord a victory dance, praising **God** that I was healed by the stripes of **Jesus**. I went to bed that night hurting worse than ever. All night I tossed and turned and moaned, all the while thanking **God** that I was not going to die but that I was healed. I got up the next morning, and all of the tumors and pain were gone. They have never come back.

And he said, Let me go, for the day breaketh. And he said I will not let thee go, except thou bless me. And he said unto him, What is thy name? And he said, Jacob. And he said, Thy name shall be called no more Jacob, but Israel: for as a prince hast thou power with God and with men, and hast prevailed (Genesis 32:26-28).

Stop Saying You Can't Remember

One morning as I was in prayer, it seemed like as if Scriptures I had memorized had simply disappeared from my mind. I was so upset that I could not quote from Scriptures I said to my wife: Honey I think I'm beginning to forget Scriptures.

She did not respond. The next time I went to quote Scriptures, it was worse than the time before. I reemphasized to my wife that I was forgetting Scriptures.

This seemed to go on for several weeks, and before I knew what was happening, I was no longer able to not just quote Scriptures, but memorize them.

One day as I was in prayer, I was complaining to the Lord. I said Lord: I'm losing my memory, and I can't remember Scriptures. Out of the blue, I heard the Lord very strongly speak into my heart with almost an audible **Voice**: you are simply Getting What You're Saying.

CHAPTER EIGHT

THE MAKING OF THE SHOFAR

#11 HORN has a Hole Drilled through It

Now the **HORN** has to have a hole drilled carefully straight through to the empty part of the **HORN**. It has to go all the way through. The **Spirit** of **God** drills carefully because it's a very precarious operation. He has to drill a perfect round hole. The

TRUMPET MUST have a clear path all the way from the beginning to the end. This will take your total cooperation. It is way more serious than a major Heart operation.

God is drilling into the deep parts of our life, in the secret parts of our life, and not just the obvious parts. He is working on the inside of us in ways that no one can see. He's drilling inside of you. He's working in you for his perfect will to be done.

When he has complete this task, you will be a **TRUMPET** that the wind of **God** blows through **FREELEY**! As **God** by the wind of His **Spirit** moves through you, it will make the inhabitants of the earth tremble, including the believers. The sound coming out of your mouth will call people who are sick to be healed, the backsliders to repent, those who love Christ, to go deeper. The wind coming out by the **Spirit** will produce Miracles and Victory!

God is trying to get you into a place where the **Spirit** of **God** speaks through you with no mixture of flesh! He can minister through you freely as He wills. He can bring life through the words you speak — words of encouragement, words of strength, words of healing, words of deliverance.

John 6:63 It is the Spirit that quickeneth; the flesh profiteth nothing: the words that I speak unto you, they are Spirit, and they are life.

2 Peter 1:19 We have also a more sure word of prophecy; whereunto ye do well that ye take heed, as unto a light that shineth in a dark place, until the day dawn, and the day star arise in your hearts:20 knowing this first, that no prophecy of the scripture is of any private interpretation.:21 For the prophecy came not in old time by the will of man: but holy

men of God spake as they were moved by the Holy Ghost.

The **Spirit** of **God** was singing through **Jesus**, his lips of clay, songs that brought complete and total healing to those who had ears to hear! Now his **HORN** was straight as an arrow. There were no twist or turns in him. Flesh never hindered the move of **God** in his life. There was no limit to the flow of **God**s Wind, His **Spirit**!

John 3:34 For he whom God hath sent speaketh the words of God: for God giveth not the Spirit by measure unto him.

Romans 1:4 and declared to be the Son of God with power, according to the Spirit of holiness, by the resurrection from the dead:

Our problem is that this hole most times that runs through us is so small and clogged that the **Holy Spirit** can very seldom blow through us. And when He does, there is still so much flesh that the sound that comes out is out of **Tune** and distorted. The cartridge that has not been completely dealt with comes flying out of the end of the **HORN** like spittle out of some one's mouth which is overexcited.

Ephesians 4:28 Let him that stole steal no more: but rather let him labor, working with his hands the thing which is good, that he may have to give to him that needeth. 29 Let no corrupt communication proceed out of your mouth, but that which is good to the use of edifying, that it may minister grace unto the hearers. 30 And grieve not the Holy Spirit of God, whereby ye are sealed unto the day of redemption.

Colossians 4:6 Let your speech be always with grace, seasoned with salt, that ye may know how ye ought to answer every man.

Ecclesiastes 10:12 The words of a wise man's mouth are gracious; but the lips of a fool will swallow up himself.

Proverbs 15:7 The lips of the wise disperse knowledge: but the heart of the foolish doeth not so.

Colossians 3:8 But now ye also put off all these; anger, wrath, malice, blasphemy, filthy communication out of your mouth.9 Lie not one to another, seeing that ye have put off the old man with his deeds;

James 3:2 For in many things we offend all. If any man offend not in word, the same is a perfect man, and able also to bridle the whole body.3 Behold, we put bits in the horses' mouths, that they may obey us; and we turn about their whole body.4 Behold also the ships, which though they be so great, and are driven of fierce winds, yet are they turned about with a very small helm, whithersoever the governor listeth.

Proverbs 15:4 A wholesome tongue is a tree of life: but perverseness therein is a breach in the Spirit.

Psalm 37:30 The mouth of the righteous speaketh wisdom, and his tongue talketh of judgment.31 The law of his God is in his heart; none of his steps shall slide.

Ephesians 5:3 But fornication, and all uncleanness, or covetousness, let it not be once named among you, as becometh saints;4 Neither filthiness, nor foolish talking, nor jesting, which are not convenient: but rather giving of thanks.

Colossians 3:16-17 King James Version (KJV)
16 Let the word of Christ dwell in you richly in all wisdom; teaching and admonishing one another in psalms and hymns and Spiritual songs, singing with grace in your hearts to the Lord.17 And whatsoever ye do in word or deed, do all in the name of the Lord Jesus, giving thanks to God and the Father by him.

Luke 4:22 And all bare him witness, and wondered at the gracious words which proceeded out of his mouth. And they said, Is not this Joseph's son?

Proverbs 16:21 The wise in heart shall be called prudent: and the sweetness of the lips increaseth learning.

Isaiah 50:4 The Lord God hath given me the tongue of the learned, that I should know how to speak a word in season to him that is weary: he wakeneth morning by morning, he wakeneth mine ear to hear as the learned.

There are times that the Wind of the **Spirit** will give us prophetic words that will help us in the **Spirit**ual battles that we encounter in daily living. Paul told Timothy: by these prophetic words, he could fight a good fight in the midst of his battles. **God** knows what we are going to be going through, even in the real dark times of our lives. Yet **God** will give to us a prophetic word that will give us direction and encouragement. This prophetic word might come to you in a time of prayer, dreams, or by other people. Here is an example. I gave a prophetic word one time to a husband and a wife who were members of the church I was the pastor of.

I Prophesied in Three Days!

In one particular service, there was a married couple who had come forward for prayer. The husband and wife were both working for a youth and children s camp ministry. He was a rodeo clown for the children s camp. As I came to this couple, the **Spirit** of **God** quickened me, and I prophesied by the **Spirit** of the Lord that in three days, he would lose his job and position with that ministry. I also told them prophetically that at the time it would seem to be devastating, but that he should not despair, because **God** was about to open up new doors of opportunity for him and his family.

Sure enough just as I prophesied, within three days they called him into a meeting. In this meeting, they informed him that they were going to let him go. He was **FIRE**d right there on the spot! They **FIRE**d him because he and his wife spoke in tongues, and this ministry they work for was not a Pentecostal or full Gospel ministry.

Yes, it was extremely devastating for them, but because the Lord had already told them that this was going to happen and that they were going to have a bright and prosperous future, with a new occupation, they were able to endure this trial. **God** supernaturally gave this man and his wife favor, and they opened up another business that became prosperous.

Now prophetic words do not always pertain to the future. In the midst of this prophetic word, you might discover the operation of the **word of knowledge**, a **word of wisdom**, or the **discerning of Spirits**. All of these gifts of the **Spirit** work together by the one and same **Holy Spirit**. Holy men of **God** spoke as they were moved by the Holy Ghost. These men did not have their own agenda, they were not in it for financial rewards, and they were not looking for positions, power, prestige, or recognition! These were men of **God** who simply wanted nothing but the will of **God**. **SHOFAR**s prepared for the **Master'**s use.

Jesus himself never did anything without the **Father'**s influence and direction. Every word, deed, and action that **Jesus** took was underneath the direct leading of the **Spirit** of **God**. Christ is our supreme example of how we are to talk, walk, and live our lives in this world. The greatest challenge of our faith is to be led by the **Spirit** of **God**, moment by moment. It is so easy to get out of **God**'s will, especially when you do not have a desire to be led by the **Spirit**. For as many as are led by the **Spirit** of **God**, they are the sons of **God**. That means they are the mature, **Spirit**-filled, **God** inspired believers.

He became a Reprobate and an Outlaw

One Sunday morning, the **Spirit** of **God** moved in our service in a powerful and amazing way. Many people came forward to be prayed for that particular morning. Now in the prayer line, there was a young evangelist who had been attending our church for some time. This particular morning the **Spirit** of prophecy was flowing like a mighty river. I came up to this young man, and I laid my hands upon him, in which he immediately fell under the power of **God**.

I continued to go down the line ministering to the people. When I was about three people down from him, the **Spirit** of **God** arrested me and took hold of me. I found myself back at this man's feet. I ended up straddling him with my left foot on his right side, and my right foot on his left side. Then I reached down and grabbed his shirt with my left hand. With my right hand, I began to slap his face very hard. I must have slapped him at least five times, on both sides of his cheeks. I was not truly aware of what I was doing in the natural. It was the mighty river of **God** flowing through my innermost being.

When I am in this place of the **Spirit,** I am not leaning at all upon my natural intellect or mind. When I was done slapping him, I went back to praying for the other people.

After a brief period once again, the **Spirit** of **God** arrested me, he took me back to this young evangelist once again. I spoke by the **Spirit** of **God** to him. The **Spirit** of the Lord told him, "Even as my servant has slapped your flesh, so you must slap your flesh. If you do not crucify your flesh, you will become a reprobate to the gospel and a fugitive from the law!" Now when the **Spirit** of **God** moves upon me this way, I sometimes do not completely remember the things that I say.

Three days later, I received a phone call from one of the ladies in the church. She was weeping and said that her twenty-some-year-old daughter had up and ran away with this particular evangelist. Not only had this young evangelist ran away with this lady's daughter, but it turned out that he was also involved with another young lady in the church. It was revealed that they had been involved in a sexual relationship also. I prayed with her over the phone.

Approximately one month later, I received another phone call from this same lady whose daughter had run away with this evangelist. She informed me that her daughter had been being beaten by this man and that they had gone out one-night drinking when they were pulled over by a policeman. This evangelist got in an argument with the officer, which ended up with him physically fighting this policeman.

Before he knew what he was doing, he had grabbed the police officer's revolver out of his holster and aimed the gun at the cop. He then left her daughter and the police officer and ran for his life. Supposedly, he was headed for Canada. The last time I had heard, he was a fugitive of the law. Now I cannot verify all of this story; this is simply what was told me by the girl's mother. According to her story, everything that I had prophesied over this young evangelist if you did not crucify his flesh came to pass. If only we would harken to the correction of **God**'s **Voice** and **Spirit**, how much trouble and disaster we could prevent. May **God** have mercy on us!

Three Precise Prophecies came to Pass!

One of the mothers in the church (Mary) came to the front for prayer. The **Spirit** of the Lord quickened me, and I prophesied that all of her children would be saved. I also said and that her husband would also be saved, but it would be as if he was snatched from the flames of hell. Several years later, she shared with me that everything I said came to pass. Her husband ended up with cancer. He was not open to the things of **God**, but as he lay on the bed of death, he cried out to **Jesus**. He was gloriously saved, with deep hunger for the things of **God**. Shortly after that, he slipped off into eternity. He had been snatched from the flames of hell. Here is her story in her own words.

Mary's Testimony: My name is Mary J. Rockwell. I would like to share three quick testimonies in which I saw **God** speak in precise and prophetic, powerful ways in connection to Pastor Mike:

Testimony 1: Years ago, my mother was very sick and in the hospital in New York state. I had asked Pastor Mike to pray for me before leaving Maryland to go see her. He told me when I saw her; I was to pray over her and say, "I command all tormenting mental **Spirit**s to leave her now in the name of **Jesus**. He said that after I spoke this word of authority in the name of **Jesus,** then I was to Clap my hands together three times and say: Now!

When I arrived at the hospital, three of her doctors told me that she was going to die. My sister had called a pastor and began planning for her funeral. She had not eaten for days and had huge bags of fluid in the whites of her eyes and all over her face and didn't even look human. She was in a coma-like condition. She was hooked up to IVs and monitors.

I waited until she and I were the only ones left in the room. I pulled the curtain around us, put my hands on her head, and prayed and commanded just as the Lord told me to according to the prophetic word from Pastor Mike. Then I clapped my hands three times, and I said, **"Now."** As I did this, I felt a surge leave my hands and go into her body. The next morning I went in to see her. The IVs had been removed, and she had come out of her coma. She was eating, and all the pockets of fluid had disappeared from her face and eyes! The doctors were amazed because according to all of their medical knowledge, she should've been dead. They released her that morning. She lived another three or four years.

Testimony 2: I had fallen and broken both my wrists. The doctor had put a cast on one, but I wouldn't let him cast the other. I went to Pastor Mike's home, and he met me in the driveway. I asked him to pray for my healing, so he did. He told me prophetically that I was healed. I went home, and within a week, I felt that my wrists were healed. I told the doctor either he remove the cast or I would have my husband cut it off. The doctor had told me I would have to keep it on for weeks, but he reluctantly removed it. That same week I painted three ceilings by hand. The Lord had healed my wrists!

Testimony 3: When my children were still in school, I went up to the altar for prayer. Pastor Mike prayed and said, "Your prayers have reached the very throne room of heaven. **God** said, "You will live to see all of your children serve the Lord. Your husband will be saved, but he will be pulled out of the pit of hell at the very end." My husband, at age seventy-two, contracted cancer from exposure to deadly chemicals while serving in the Marines in Vietnam. I had assumed that he knew the Lord. I prayed for him and said, "I could lay hands on you until you are bald, but you need to cry out to **Jesus** for yourself." He could not say the name, **Jesu,** so I knew instantly that it was a demonic block. That it was obvious he was not yet born again.

I called a local pastor and was about to relate that to him when he told me that my husband's perception of salvation was wrong, and he didn't believe he was saved. He went to the hospital and prayed with him. My husband called me on the phone and said he had just received **Jesus** Christ as his Lord and Savior.

His one regret was that he hadn't done enough for the Lord. The Lord had spoken to two young ladies who lived miles away from us to come and pray with him. When they came, my husband prayed for them, and they wept and wept. It was not very long after that that he went home to be with the Lord. It was even as Pastor Mike prophesied. He was snatched out of the flames of the pit of hell right at the end of his life.

Three people who were there when Pastor Mike prayed for me called me on the phone, and each of them reminded me of the prayer that Pastor Mike had prayed over me many years before that. Each of them inquired if my husband was saved, and I told them it was just as Pastor Mike had prayed many years before. Since then, two of my four children are serving the Lord...two more to go!

Prophetic Word That I Gave Saved Him $45,000

I had a precious brother who came to me the other day and made a bold statement. He declared, you saved me $45,000. I was surprised that he made this statement. I said to him, what exactly are you talking about? He told me that right before the economy fell through that, I gave him a prophetic word that he needed to trade in his 401(k)! Honestly, I did not even know that he had any 401(k)s. I do not even remember prophesying this to him.

Many times this is the case when I am moving in the **Spirit**, I will make statements or give prophetic words to people and not remember what I said. This is probably for the best, that way I cannot take the glory for myself. This brother had plenty of experiences with me as his pastor, though, so he took to heart what I said to him. He told me that he immediately went and cashed in his 401(k)s. He also informed me that he was extremely glad that he had listened to the prophetic word because if he had waited any longer, he would have lost $45,000. It is so important that we hear from heaven in order to preserve our lives.

Prophesied to a Brother his family would Re-unite!

One day I received a phone call from a gentleman who wanted to rent a room from me. I have a house where I keep single men, helping them to get back on their feet. As I was speaking to him, he told me he knew who I was. I asked him: how's that? He informed me that several years ago, he had visited our church. When he began to describe to me his family, immediately I remembered him. He came to our church with his family all dressed up, in a strict religious style.

At the end of that service, he informed me in his opinion that our church would never grow. I asked him why he would say such a thing. He said: if you were preaching a religious and even restrictive philosophy, there would be a chance of growth. But because you are preaching the divine nature of Christ, the fruits of the **Spirit**, and the character of **God**, true holiness of the heart, most who come will not stay. He told me people like religion they can take pride in. That was the last time I had seen him or his family.

Now here he was some years later. He informed me that he had lost his wife, and his children were scattered. Three sons and a daughter were spread out among relatives. He had fallen back into drugs and alcohol, going astray. As I was speaking to him, the

Spirit of the Lord gave me a word of wisdom. I told him by a prophetic word of the Lord, "I will rent a room to you at the house that is located on the church's property. Your wife will come back in approximately a month, then your children will come home, and your family will be restored." I told him to begin to attend our services, cry out to **God**, and he will answer you.

He moved into the room that I had made available, with no security or money. I knew that **God** wanted to do a miracle for him and his family. He began to attend our services. Approximately three Sundays later, his wife shows up at one of our services. She had her hair dyed black, with black mascara on her eyes, looking Gothic. I was not moved by her rough appearance, for I had heard the word of the Lord. During the time of preaching and teaching, the **Spirit** of **God** moved on her in a mighty way. She began to cry, with mascara running down her face. When I gave the altar call, she responded wholeheartedly. Oh, what a wonderful and beautiful instant change we saw in her.

She started coming to the services, and we saw her aggressively going after **God**. During the worship time, she would be standing on her tippy toes; her arms stretched towards heaven, tears rolling down her face, hungry for **Jesus**. In a very short time, all of the Gothic dress was completely gone. Within a very short time, they had gathered all their children back to themselves. I rented an apartment for them, which had four bedrooms. **God** had restored his family, even as I had prophesied by the **Spirit** of the Lord.

During this period we ended up opening up a thrift store, where his wife would work through the day. Her husband, when he was not seeking work, or doing work, would help at this thrift store. My children grew close to their children, many times babysitting them when the parents went away. **God** is so good and is more than willing to give us opportunity after opportunity to get right with him. He wants to restore every family. He wants to heal every marriage. He wants to set the captives free. We have a choice whether or not we will follow Christ or forsake him, and go our own way.

He Did Not Have to Die!

One night (back in 1975) while I was praying alone in my barracks, when a holy Prophetic unction and urgency came upon me to pray for a Muslim man that I knew. As I responded to this unction of the Holy Ghost, I entered into deep travail for his soul. I began to weep almost uncontrollably for this man, whose name was Hussein. He was a military friend of mine whom that I used to do drugs with.

As I prayed, the Prophetic **Spirit** of **God** spoke to my heart, telling me: **the devil was going to kill him very shortly if he did not repent, and cry out to Jesus. The Spirit of God told me that Hussein had only a very short period of time left on the earth before the enemy would snuff out his precious life.**

This unction, this deep urgency of **God** was so strong within me that I got up off of the floor of my dorm room, where I had been praying. I immediately went to his room and knocked on his door. Hussein opened his door and saw me standing there weeping uncontrollably. I was so moved in my heart that I could not speak for a while. He asked what was wrong with great concern in his **Voice**. “Mike, Mike, what’s wrong?” I could barely speak in English because I was weeping so hard.

I finally was able to tell him that I had been in prayer in my room when the **Spirit** of **God** told me that the devil was about to kill him. I told him that his time to get right with the Lord was running out. I explained that he was going to be dead in the very near future, and that he would end up in hell without Christ. I began to plead with him with great urgency and compassion, with tears flowing down my face to get right with **God**. I encouraged him to cry out to **God**, repent for his sins, and give his heart to **Jesus** Christ.

It was obvious the **Spirit** of **God** was moving upon him in a very real way. He said that he believed what I was saying was true, but that he just was not ready to make that kind of commitment at this time. Soon after this experience, I left the Navy, headed out to minister to the Yupik Indians. I kept in touch with some of the people that I knew on this military base.

It was approximately two months later that I was speaking to one of my friends on the base when he asked me if I had heard about what happened to Hussein. I informed him, no that I had not heard anything. He told me that they had discovered him dead, with his head in the toilet. They think that he had either gotten his hands on some bad drugs or he had simply overdosed. Oh, how it must break the heart of **God** when souls are lost because they will not respond to his love and beckoning call.

THE MAKING OF THE SHOFAR

#12 In the FIRE Again

Once again the **HORN** must go through the **FIRE** to expand the hole which was drilled to where the Tipp used to be! All obstacles must be cleared out of the way. It must be prepared for use on the inside and the outside.

In the beginning, the **FIRE** was on the outside, but now the **FIRE** goes up into the inside of the **HORN**. When you see Ram's **HORN**s before all of these steps, you'll see them twisted, ugly, stinky, and in some areas, they are almost flat. Do you know what the **FIRE** does as it flows through the complete interior? It swells the **HORN**, the flatness disappears, and it becomes round, and it opens up. It burns out the stink.

There is supposed to be a FIRE burning in your soul, a passion, a longing, a hunger for God that opens you up to the moving of the Spirit.

It goes through the most radical and transformational process it has yet experienced. This **HORN** will never look the same, smell the same, and sound the same. If you would hold up the original version next to the new version you would not know that it is the same Rams **HORN**! This Baptism of **FIRE** has almost completed the process!

Baptism of FIRE

In the Bible, '**FIRE**' is sometimes used as an image of destruction. It is also used to symbolize passion, power, and purity. Oh, how we need a baptism of **FIRE**. Oh, we need a Holy Ghost **FIRE** burning in us. You know, **God** said is not my word like a hammer, like a **FIRE** that burns up the stubble. The **FIRE** has to be in us and just on the exterior. It is **God**'s presence because **God** is a consuming **FIRE**.

Matthew 3:11, John the Baptist said: 'I indeed baptize you in water unto repentance: but he that cometh after me is mightier than I, whose shoes I am not worthy to bear: he shall baptize you in the Holy Spirit and FIRE.' A Christian brother recently identified this 'FIRE' with the outpouring of the Spirit on Pentecost. Would you comment on this?"

Matthew 3:11, John the Baptist said: 'I indeed baptize you in water unto repentance: but he that cometh after me is mightier than I, whose shoes I am not worthy to bear: he shall baptize you in the Holy Spirit and FIRE.' A Christian brother recently identified this 'FIRE' with the outpouring of the Spirit on Pentecost. Would you comment on this?"

If you study the New Testament, there are three different baptisms!

#1 Being Baptized in Water

#2 Being Baptized in the Holy Ghost

#3 The Baptism of FIRE

Baptism in the Holy Ghost and baptism in the **FIRE** of **God** are two different baptisms.

By faith, we received the baptism of the Holy Ghost. The initial evidence is speaking in a heavenly language. What happened on the day of Pentecost was more than just the baptism of the Holy Ghost. They also experienced a baptismal of **FIRE**.

Acts 1:8: But you shall receive power, after that the Holy Ghost is come upon you: and you shall be witnesses unto me both in Jerusalem, and in all Judaea, and in Samaria, and unto the uttermost part of the earth.

This baptismal of **FIRE** does not happen to every believer. It is not because it's not available; it's just that many do not desire it. This baptism of **FIRE** will purge and cleanse a person from the inside out. This **Holy Spirit FIRE** burns with a fervent heat on the inside of you, and you experience it. This baptism of **FIRE** is meant for the ministry and carrying out the great commission.

When this **FIRE** gets into a person, that person's life changes at that very instance. Everything in the world becomes valueless, even his/her own life, and his/her total focus becomes **Jesus** Christ and carrying out the great commission. At this point, dying for the ministry is not an issue, and one is ready to be persecuted (die) for the gospel.

It is a **FIRE** burning inside of a believer that burns very bright. All s/he thinks, needs and wants is to preach and teach **Jesus** Christ. When this baptism of **FIRE** comes, the wind of the Holy Ghost will sound for through your **TRUMPET**. You open your mouth to preach, teach, proclaim, and the words of the Holy Ghost just flow out of your belly like rivers of living water. At this point, it is the **Holy Spirit** speaking, not the person; the person is just a vessel being used.

It is when a person is in this condition that they will experience miracles, healings, mighty signs, and wonders to where the dead will even be raised. When you are baptized with **FIRE**, the only thing you want to do is to minister and preach the gospel. You, Will, find yourself in the streets, roads, and everywhere you find opportunities to preach the gospel. (Some of this information came from non-copyrighted material on the Internet)

Refiners FIRE

Malachi 3:1"Behold, I send my messenger, and he will prepare the way before me. And the Lord whom you seek will suddenly come to his temple; and the messenger of the covenant in whom you delight, behold, he is coming, says the Lord of hosts. But who can endure the day of his coming, and who can stand when he appears? For he is like a refiner's FIRE and like fullers' soap. He will sit as a refiner and purifier of silver, and he will purify the sons of Levi and refine them like gold and silver, and they will bring offerings in righteousness to the Lord.

Malachi says that, when the Lord returns, no one will be able to stand before Him. The Lord's holiness and judgment will be as a refiner's blazing **FIRE** and as a fuller's soap. The idea of "standing" before the Lord is dealing with the sinful flesh and will not be able to resist the Lord in His glory.

Malachi 3:2 says the Messiah will be like a refiner's **FIRE**, a reference to the process of purifying the metal. A refiner uses a **FIRE** to heat the metal to a molten state; then he skims off the dross that floats to the top. The refiner's **FIRE** is, of course, maintained at an extremely high temperature, and such a high degree of heat is the prophet's picture of the people will face at the coming of Christ. All judgment has been entrusted to the Son (John 5:22).

Second, the Messiah will be like a launderer's soap. This type of soap was quite effective in producing bright white clothing. The HCSB translates it as "cleansing lye." The coming of Christ was to cleanse Believers of all impurity. Every stain of sin is to be dealt with. The account of **Jesus**' transfiguration contains a reference to His purity, using language similar to Malachi's: "He was transfigured before them. His clothes became dazzling white, whiter than anyone in the world could bleach them" (Mark 9:2–3). It is the purpose of **God** that His people are to take the Likeness and Image of Christ.

The goal of **Jesus** will be to judge wickedness and purify His people: "He will sit as a refiner and purifier of silver; he will purify the Levites and refine them like gold and silver. Then the LORD will have men who will bring offerings in righteousness" (Malachi 3:3).

Like the refiner's **FIRE**, He will burn away the impurities of His people. Like launderer's soap, He will wash away their uncleanness (Deuteronomy 4:29; Isaiah 1:25; Jeremiah 6:29–30; Ezekiel 22:17–22; Zechariah 3:5). **Jesus** desires to create a pure heart.

The refiner's **FIRE** and launderer's soap indicate the holiness and burning judgment of the Messiah. His purifying brightness and absolute holiness will affect those who serve Him, creating a cleansed temple and purified priesthood.

SMITH WIGGLESWORTH & FIRE

Smith - "Repeat in your heart often: "baptized with the Holy Ghost and FIRE, FIRE, FIRE!" All the unction, and weeping, and travailing comes through the baptism of FIRE, and I say to you and say to myself, purged and cleansed and filled with renewed Spiritual power." "Who makes his ministers a flame of FIRE." Heb. 1:7

"If you want to increase in the life of **God**, then you must settle it in your heart that you will not at any time resist the **Holy Spirit**. The Holy Ghost and **FIRE** - the **FIRE is** burning up everything that would impoverish and destroy you."

I was about to leave Sunderland. This revival was taking place in the vestry of an Episcopal Church. I went to the parsonage that day to say goodbye, and I said to Sister Boddy, the vicar's wife, "I am going away, but I have not received the tongues yet." She said, "It isn't tongues you need, but the Baptism." I said, "I have the Baptism, Sister, but I would like to have you lay hands on me before I leave."

She laid her hands on me and then had to go out of the room. The **FIRE** fell. It was a wonderful time as I was there with **God** alone. It seemed as though **God** bathed me in power. I was given a wonderful vision. I was conscious of the cleansing of the precious blood and cried out, "Clean! Clean! Clean!" I was filled with the joy of the consciousness of the cleansing. I saw the Lord **Jesus** Christ.

I saw the empty cross and I saw Him exalted at the right hand of **God** the **Father**. As I was extolling, magnifying, and praising Him, I was speaking in tongues as the **Spirit** of **God** gave me utterance. I knew now that I had received the real Baptism in the

Holy Ghost. When I got home, my wife said to me, "So you think you have received the Baptism of the Holy Ghost. Why I am as much baptized in the Holy Ghost as you are." We had sat on the platform together for twenty years, but that night, she said, "Tonight, you will be preaching to the congregation." I said, "All right."

As I went up to the platform that night, the Lord gave me the first few verses of the sixty-first chapter of Isaiah. "The **Spirit** of the Lord **God** is upon me; because the Lord hath anointed me to preach good tidings unto the meek: He hath sent me to bind up the broken-hearted, to proclaim liberty to the captives, and the opening of the prison to them that are bound."

My wife went back to one of the furthermost seats in the hall, and she said to herself, "I will watch what happens." I preached that night on the subject the Lord had given me, and I told what the Lord had done for me. I told the people that I was going to have **God** in my life, and I would gladly suffer a thousand deaths rather than forfeit this wonderful infilling that had come to me.

My wife was very restless. She was moved in a new way and said, "That is not my Smith that is preaching. Lord, you have done something for him." As soon as I had finished, the secretary of the mission got up and said, "Brethren, I want what the leader of our mission has got."

He tried to sit down but missed his seat and fell on the floor. There were soon fourteen of them on the floor, my wife included. We did not know what to do, but the Holy Ghost got hold of the situation, and the **FIRE** fell. A revival started, and the crowds came. It was only the beginning of the flood-tide of blessing. We had touched the reservoir of the Lord's life and power. Since that time, the Lord has taken me to many different lands, and I have witnessed many blessed outpourings of **God**'s **Holy Spirit**.

I was traveling from Egypt to Italy. **God** was visiting me wonderfully on this ship, and every hour, I was conscious of His blessed presence. A man on the ship suddenly collapsed, and his wife was terribly alarmed, and everybody else was panicking. Some said that he was about to expire. But I saw it was just a glorious opportunity for the power of **God** to be manifested. Oh, what it means to be a flame of **FIRE**, to be indwelt by the living Christ!

We are in bad condition if we have to pray for power when an occasion like this comes along, or if we have to wait until we feel a sense of His presence.

The Lord's promise was, "Ye shall receive power after that the Holy Ghost comes upon you," and if we will believe, the power of **God** will always be manifested when there is a definite need. When you exercise your faith, you will find that there is greater power in you than that is in the world.

Oh, to be awakened out of unbelief into a place of daring for **God** on the authority of His blessed Book and the redemptive work of Christ!

So right there on board that ship, in the name of **Jesus,** I rebuked the devil, and to the astonishment of the man's wife and the man himself, he was able to stand. He said, "What is this? It is going all over me. I have never felt anything like this before." From the top of his head to the soles of his feet, the power of **God** shook him. **God** has given us authority over all the power of the devil. Oh, that we may live in the place where we realize this always, and that was completely submitted to that authority!

We need to have something more than smoke and huff and puff to touch the people; we need to be a burning **FIRE** for **God**. His ministers must be flames of **FIRE**. In those days, there were thousands out to hear the Word of **God**. I believe there were about three thousand persons crying for mercy at once that day. It was a great sight.

From that first morning on the meetings grew to such an extent that I would estimate every time some 5,000 to 6,000 gathered, and I had to preach in temperatures of 110 degrees. Then I had to pray for these sick people. But I can tell you, a flame of **FIRE** can do anything. Things change in the **FIRE**. This was Pentecost. But what moved me more than anything else was this: there were hundreds who tried to touch me, they were so impressed with the power of **God** that was present. And many testified that with the touch they were healed, It was not that there was any virtue in me—the people's faith was exercised as it was at Jerusalem when they said Peter's shadow would heal them.

A preacher, suffering many days from the kick of a horse, walking with great pain and in much distress, made a special call at the hotel in which I was staying, and being led by the **Spirit**, according to **God**'s Word, I laid hands on the bruised ankle. A **FIRE** broke out with burning and healing power, and from that moment on, he could walk easily and without pain.

Ralph Darling on FIRE for God

(From Author)

One day a tall, middle-aged man came into our church service. His wife came with him. They came for help because they were having trouble in their marriage. The Lord allowed me to minister to them both. The Holy Ghost moved upon them in a mighty way. I had the privilege of leading Ralph into the baptism of the Holy Ghost with speaking in tongues.

From that minute forward Ralph Darling was never the same. He was on **FIRE** for **God**. Ralph, Paul, and I would go to carnivals whenever they were in the area. We would carry bags of tracks with us to share with others. They were comic book tracks I had a tremendous effect. I'm not exaggerating when I would say that we have given away tens of thousands of these tracks through the years.

Even after we left the three Springs Assembly of **God** Church, Ralph and Paul kept on evangelizing. My wife and I were in Germany for about nine months. When we came back to the USA, we heard the bad news. Ralph had come down with cancer. He was on the edge of death. He told his wife Peggy that he was ready to go home to be with the Lord. My wife and I did swing by to see him and to pray with him. One night as Kathy and I were gone ministering at another gospel meeting, Ralph went home into the arms of **Jesus**.

Paul weight, who was there told us the story. He said: Ralph was lying in bed propped up by pillows. He said goodbye to Peggy and Paul. Then he lifted his hands towards heaven and began to worship the Lord. With his hands lifted towards heaven Ralph left his body to be ever with the Lord.

Alvin Raised from the Bed of Death

One morning I received a phone call from my good friend, Paul. He told me that he knew of a man who owned a logging company and lumber yard who was about to die. They were waiting for him to expire any day because his body was filled with cancer. Most of it was concentrated in his chest, and it had spread throughout the rest of his body. He was located in the McConnell burg hospital. Paul asked me if I would be willing to go pray for him. I asked him to give me one day to fast and pray for this particular situation. I spent the rest of that day in prayer, fasting, and in the Word.

The next morning Paul came to pick me up. We drove up to the McConnell burg hospital, praying as we went. We walked into the foyer and up to the information desk. The nurse gave us the necessary information we needed. Paul said he would wait for me and that he would continue in prayer in the hospital's chapel. I found the room where they had put this gentleman, knocked on the door, and entered.

They had placed him in a very small room—just big enough to be a closet—that was off the beaten path like they were just waiting for him to die. He was lying on a hospital bed and was nothing but skin and bones; he looked as if he had just come out of a concentration camp. His skin and the whites of his eyes were yellow. He was a rather tall man who looked to be in his late sixties. He was lying on his bed, wide awake. I had no idea what his mental condition was. I began to speak to him and discovered he was aware of his surroundings, and actually, I was amazed at how clear and quick his mind was.

I began to speak to him by introducing myself. He almost seemed to take an antagonistic attitude towards me right away. I began to share **Jesus** with him, but as I was speaking to him, a smirk appeared on his face. He began to tell me stories of the things he had seen in church— supernatural things. He said one time he was in a wild church service where everybody was jumping and shouting.

It was several years ago, and they did not yet have electricity in this church. He said as he was watching people dance and shout, one of them jumped so high that he hit a lighted kerosene lantern, causing it to fall off of the hook. It came crashing down onto the floor and should have immediately broken into pieces and caught the building on **FIRE**. Instead, he said it almost acted like a ball. It never broke or went out but landed straight up. The people just kept on dancing and singing to the Lord.

After he told me this story, he looked me right in the eyes and said to me, "If I did not get saved back then, what makes you think you are going to get me saved now?" I did not answer him. My heart was filled with deep sorrow and overwhelming love for him. I knew I could not help him, and if was going to get saved and be healed, it was going to take **God** moving upon him supernaturally.

I stepped away from his deathbed, and I bowed my head and cried out to **God**. "Lord, touch this man, help me to reach him because I cannot do it within myself. Lord, you're going to have to touch his heart, or he will lose his soul and end up in hell." As I was praying under my breath, I sensed the awesome presence of **God** come flooding into that little hospital room.

Then the **Spirit** of the Lord rose up within me, and I walked back over to his bed. I began to speak to Elvin once again, but it was under a divine unction of great compassion. I know I did not say very much, but as I was speaking, all of a sudden out of the blue, he began to weep uncontrollably. In just a matter of seconds, his heart was completely open to the gospel. He gave his heart to **Jesus** Christ right then and there. Then I laid my hands on him and commanded his body to be healed. I rebuked the **Spirit** of death, and cancer in the name of **Jesus** Christ, commanding it to go.

When I was done praying, it seemed to me there was some immediate improvement in his countenance and body. I told him as I got ready to leave that I would visit him again in the hospital. After I left something wonderful happened, but I did not hear the story until later that day when I arrived home from the hospital.

Immediately Elvin felt healed in his body. His appetite came back, and yellow jaundice disappeared completely from his skin and from the white of his eyes. The hospital personnel was amazed at this transformation. They took some new x-rays and discovered that the cancer he had in his body was almost totally gone. Cancer that was in his lungs which had been the size of a baseball was now the size of a cashew nut. In three days' time they released him from the hospital and sent him home. He was working at his sawmill with his son and grandsons within a week!

Jesus saith unto him, Rise, take up thy bed, and walk. And immediately the man was made whole, and took up his bed, and walked: and on the same day was the Sabbath (John 5:8-9).

A Mighty Move among the Methodist

One Wednesday night close to a dozen young people came into our church service. When I say young, they were about my age, or just a little bit younger. I was 24 years old at the time. They were a group of people that were extremely hungry for **God**. I think there was approximately a dozen of them.

The Lord gave me the privilege of leading many of them into the baptism of the Holy Ghost. As a result of the Lord moving upon their hearts, they got permission from their Methodist pastor to let me speak in their church in Houston town. The **Spirit** of **God** moved in a mighty way in that meeting.

It was not long after my wife, and I left for Germany, that all of these young people started a new church that was hungry for the moving of the Holy Ghost, which is there to this day. One of the young men Bill Chiloe became the teacher in the Bible College that the Lord had me open. Then Bill started a Church in McConnellsburg, where he is still the pastor as of 2019.

CHAPTER NINE

THE MAKING OF THE SHOFAR

Sound Adjustment

And after all that hard process, we finally reach the stage of adjusting the SHOFAR's sound! How is that done? Of course, this is also a professional secret!

The sound is adjusted by the maker according to the customers' requirements, and according to the preferences of people from the various communities. Each

Jewish ethnic community has its own preferred SHOFAR and preferred sound.

The various SHOFARs have different sounds: thick, raw, thin, and weeping. The process of making the SHOFAR and its type affect the sound it produces. (From the Internet)

#13 HORN Is Fine-Tuned

The **HORN** is flattened and given a turned up bell by applying heat to soften it. A hole is made from the tip of the **HORN** to the natural hollow inside. If a **SHOFAR** has an unintentional hole or tears affecting its sound, it becomes unfit for ceremonial use. A **SHOFAR** may not be painted with colors, but it may be carved with artistic designs.

Definition of fine-Tune
transitive verb

1a: to adjust precisely so as to bring to the highest level of performance or effectiveness

b : to improve through minor alteration or revision

When the **Craftsman** blows through this **HORN** at the beginning, it does not make a very good sound, because it is still constrained and restricted. If there are any restrictions in the **HORN,** the **Master Craftsman**'s face will turn blue as he endeavors to blow through it.

He must go back to work till it opens it up. He begins by going back to the inside. That's the craftsmen, and he begins to sand and work, and he puts his lips to the **HORN**, and he blows again. As it begins to sound better, he will begin to **Tune** it with a Hebrew song. The **Craftsman** has ears to hear. He **Tunes** it by the **FIRE** and filing over and over, till it is the perfect sound in his ears.

This is how **God** works on us. He will not stop working until He achieves the perfect Sound, **THUNDERING**'s of Heaven.

God Wants to Fine Tune us

Smith Wigglesworth
I want you all to be in a place where we receive many blessings from **God**. It is not possible for any of you to go out with pain if you would only believe **God**, the Word of **God** if you receive it tonight, it is life, it gives deliverance to every captive. I want to preach the Word tonight so that all the people will know; you will go with the knowledge of the deliverance of **God**.

I want everyone to receive a blessing at the commencement of the meeting; no one person needs to live out of the plan of **God**. If you have pain in your knee if you believe when you stand up as sure as you are there you will be free. I believe the Word of **God**. **God** has promised if we will believe we can have whatsoever we ask.

We want you to have it changed. The present tense <u>Tunes</u> are better than future tense <u>Tunes</u>. If you get full salvation, you will have a present tense <u>Tune</u>. It is a good thing to be able to hope for sometimes… but it is a better thing to have it.

Becoming The Lord's SHOFAR

I used to hope and trust I was baptized in the Holy Ghost, but, I did not speak in Tongues. I used to believe I was. You cannot move a fact by an argument, and when you get baptized in the Holy Ghost, the **Spirit** speaks through you, then you know it is done. You Know the Comforter has come. Has He come to you? Has the Comforter come to you?

You must have Him; you must be filled with the **Spirit**, you must have an overflowing because **Jesus** says after you have received the Holy Ghost ye shall have Power. We want you to have power.

Let us look at the Scriptures. Verily, verily I say that whatsoever you ask the **Father** in my name, I will do it, that the **Father** may be glorified in the Son. If ye shall ask anything in my name I will do it, I WILL DO IT, who says it? **JESUS** that blessed **Jesus**, that lovely **Jesus**, that incarnation from heaven that blessed Son of **God**.

How He wants to bless, how He saves to the uttermost, no one spoke as He spoke. How? Come unto me all ye that are weary and heavy laden and I will give you rest. Hear what **Jesus** says - I come not into the world to condemn the world, but that the world through me might be saved. How beautiful. **Jesus** wants us all to be saved. Did you ever look at Him in His sympathy? Just take a vision of Him on Mount Olives and looking over Jerusalem weeping and saying Oh Jerusalem, Oh Jerusalem how often I would have gathered thee, and you would not.

Shall it not be said of the people in Colombo, in Ceylon. How often would I have gathered thee as a hen gathered the chickens under her wings, and you would not. Will you. Hear what He said. **WHATSOEVER YE SHALL ASK IN MY NAME I WILL DO IT**. What do you want, how much do you want, do you want anything. Are you thirsty, are you hungry, Come unto me all that thirst and I will give you water of life, Are you hungry, he that eateth the flesh and drinketh the blood of the Son of man shall live for ever.

Do you want to live forever? **Jesus** who saves to the uttermost, He heals, He helps all that come to Him.

How many are coming for healing? How many for salvation? Listen - Whatsoever ye ask in my name I will do it, the Word of the living **God**, The Son of **God**. How beautifully **God** speaks of Him - This is my beloved Son, and yet He gave Himself for us, He gave Himself as a ransom for us, Amen.

How many are going to receive Him? Take the Water of Life freely. You may say, how can I take Him. Believe on the Lord **Jesus** Christ, and you shall be saved. What is it to believe. He that heareth my Word and believeth on Him that sent me hath everlasting life.

Who are the people that followed **Jesus** – they that love Him in their hearts. Do you love Him in your hearts? From this day if you do love Him, you will begin to hate all kinds of sin, and you will love all kinds of righteousness, that is the secret. The man that says he loves **God** and loves the world – he is a liar. **God** says the truth is not in him. If a man loves the world, the love of the **Father** is not in him, and you can tell tonight whether you love **God** or not. Do you love the world, then the love of the **Father** is not in you. If you hate the world, then the love of the Lord **Jesus** is in you. Hallelujah.

I want to make you love Him. Is He worth loving? What has He done? He bought salvation; He died to deliver. The wages of sin is death. The gift of **God** is eternal life.

I leave it with you. Will you love Him. Will you serve Him. Will you. He knows it, He understands.

There's no one that loves me like Jesus,
There's no one that knows me like Him,
He knows all your sickness
He knows all your problems
There's no one that knows me like Him.

That's what He says. COME UNTO ME. He knows you are needy.

I want you to be blessed now; I find I get blessed as I ask, in the street, everywhere. If you find me in the street or anywhere, if I am alone I shall be talking to **God**, I make it my business to talk to **God** all the time If I wake in the night I make it my business to pray, and that's the reason I believe that **God** keeps me right, always right, always ready. I believe that **God** the Holy Ghost keeps us living in communion with **God**.

I want you to begin now; begin talking to **God**.

PRAYER.

John 14:12.
Jesus was the way and the truth, and therefore, all that **Jesus** said was true. **Jesus** said truly, truly, if you believe greater works than these shall ye do because I go to the **Father**.

Has He gone? If I told you earthly things and left them - now I tell you heavenly things. The son of man is down, the son of man is up. This is the greatest and one of the deepest truths possible for the believer.

Do you see this Electric Light? That light is receiving power from the dynamo; it has a receiver and transmitter. The powerhouse may be a mile or two away, the wires that are conveying the current to and from are covered. Where you are getting the light is bare wire, the juice is passing through the bare wire and gives you the light.

To bring it to you tonight to understand the life in Christ. **Jesus** sends the light, and life through, and it illuminates the life then returns and just as you are holy inside, the revelation of **God** is made manifest, and the life becomes full of illumination. My life is from Him, my life receives back to Him, and I am kept by the life of **God**.

I touch them, and instantly, they change. The Life of the Son of **God** goes through and passes on. I live by the faith of the Son of **God**.

He that believeth on Me - he that believeth. The devils believe and tremble. People follow Scripture as if it had nothing to do with it. The Scripture may be Life or letter. My **Spirit** - my Word - what is the Word. It is **Spirit** and life-giving when we believe. What is believing, Believing is the asking of the divine life that **God** gives to Him. Who desires. Everyone in this place can have Divine Life.

We do not believe in baptismal regeneration. You cannot be saved by riches. **Jesus** says ye must be born again. The new birth comes through faith in the Lord **Jesus** Christ, and you can be saved in the field as well as in a church. It is the heart, when the heart desires after righteousness, **God** makes Himself known, so we want you to be saved by the Blood tonight. Someone says I want to be saved. Shall I bring you to the Word, he that asketh receiveth, who says - **Jesus** says, he that asks receives.

If I ask Him to receive me
Will, He say me nay,
Not till earth and not till heaven
Pass away.

Salvation is of the Lord. No man can save you; no man can heal you. If anyone has been healed in these meetings, it is the Lord that has healed them. I would not take it under any circumstances that I can heal anybody, but I believe His Word - He that believeth on me greater works than these shall he do because I go to my **Father**. He is lovely, Lovely **Jesus**.

He knows it all; He knows it all,
My Father knows it all,
The bitter tears how fast they fall,
He knows, my Father knows it all.

He knows it all; He knows it all,
My Father knows it all
The joy that comes that overflows

He knows, my Father knows it all.

Before I was baptized in the Holy Ghost, there were many songs I used to sing as they were written. **God** began a change, and He changed many songs. I believe **God** wants to change the Song in your heart.

He changed this song to me.

This is how it is sung: Oh then it will be glory for me
It will be glory for me. Oh, it is now Glory for me.
It is now glory for me, As now by His grace, I can look on His face,
Now it is glory, Glory for me.

THE MAKING OF THE SHOFAR

#14 Polished till the Glory Is Revealed

The last step is to go to work on the outside. The polishing of the outside until it begins to glow and the **Craftsman** can see the reflection of his face in the instrument. The **Craftsman** goes back to the outside of the **TRUMPET**, and he begins to Polish. Oh, he rubs and rubs and rubs because there is a glory in that **HORN** that has not yet been revealed.

There is a glory in that **HORN** that will come out. He rubs that **HORN** until the craftsmen can see his reflection in the shell of the **SHOFAR**. **God** wants to turn you into a glorious **TRUMPET**. Some times, after all, is complete they will wrap the **SHOFAR** in precious metals

From glory to glory even as by the Spirit of the Lord

2 Corinthians 3:17 Now the Lord is that Spirit: and where the Spirit of the Lord is, there is liberty. 18 But we all, with open face beholding as in a glass the glory of the Lord, are changed into the same image from glory to glory, even as by the Spirit of the Lord.

The Place Where God Will Show up

Smith Wigglesworth

You must come to a place of ashes, a place of helplessness, a place of wholehearted surrender where you do not refer to yourself. You have no justification of your own in regard to anything. You are prepared to be slandered, to be despised by everybody. But because of His personality in you, He reserves you for Himself because you are Godly, and He sets you on high because you have known His name (Ps. 91:14). He causes you to be the fruit of His loins and to bring forth His glory so that you will no longer rest in yourself. Your confidence will be in God. Ah, it is lovely. "The Lord is the Spirit; and where the

Spirit of the Lord is, there is liberty" (2 Cor. 3:17).

Born June 10th, 1859
Died March 4th, 1947

I need to be a new man. If any man be in Christ, he's a new creature. Old things are passed away.

Behold, all things are become new. Do not misunderstand me, **God**'s already done a lot of wonderful work in my life, but I'm not satisfied. I'm not content. I mean I have gone through a lot of this process that I am sharing with you in this book. It's been a long road, but he's still trying to get the **FIRE** to burn in me. He is still trying to get me to open up to him. He's still polishing.

He's trying to make it a where people can see **Jesus** in me. To hear the **Voice** of **Jesus** when I open my mouth. This is **God**'s divine plan for all of his people. This is His plan for your life. But you have got to cooperate.

Now you're not the **Master Craftsman**, so don't go grabbing the **HORN** next to you and thinking, I'm going to grind that man, that woman. I'm going to shape them. I'm going to put them in the **FIRE**. That's not your job. I had to find out as a pastor that my job is not to change you. My job is to let the **Spirit** of **God** to Blow through me. Whatever sound He desires to make should be the sound coming out of my mouth!

Matthew 24:31 And he shall send his angels with a great sound

of a TRUMPET, and they shall gather together his elect from the four winds, from one end of heaven to the other.

John 3:8 The wind bloweth where it listeth, and thou hearest the sound thereof, but canst not tell whence it cometh, and whither it goeth: so is every one that is born of the Spirit.

Acts 2:2 And suddenly there came a sound from heaven as of a rushing mighty wind, and it filled all the house where they were sitting.

1 Corinthians 14:8 For if the TRUMPET give an uncertain sound, who shall prepare himself to the battle?

1 Corinthians 15:52 in a moment, in the twinkling of an eye, at the last trump: for the TRUMPET shall sound, and the dead shall be raised incorruptible, and we shall be changed.

TRUMPETS IN THE HEAVENS

From all around the world are coming the reports of strange blasts of sound from the heavens. Some rumble like distant explosions or THUNDER, some blare like amplified TRUMPETs. YouTube has a full measure of videos taken from witnesses as Invisible Sky TRUMPETs THUNDER their hair raising blast in the distance. Commenters on these videos warn of the End of Days, and that this is a sign from God, but whatever the theory, the recordings of Sky TRUMPETs are sure to send a deep shiver up your spine.

REPEAT OF 14 STEPS

#1 Selection of the RAM
#2 Death of the RAM
#3 Breaking of the HORN
#4 The Cartridge Removed
#5 The Grinding of the HORN
#6 Placed into the FIRE
#7 HORN Is Straightened
#8 HORN is put In the Mold,
#9 HORN put under a stream of cold water
#10 Tip of HORN Is Cut off
#11 HORN has a Hole Drilled through It
#12 In the FIRE Again
#13 HORN Is Fine-Tuned
#14 Polished to the Glory Is Revealed

Playing the SHOFAR

The **SHOFAR** is played much like a European brass

instrument, with the player applying his lips to this hole, and causing the air column inside to vibrate. **SHOFAR**s used in Ashkenazic Jewish worship tend to have no carved mouthpiece. The player applies his lips directly to an irregular hole drilled in the tip of the **HORN**. Sephardic Jewish **SHOFAR**s, on the other hand, usually do have a carved mouthpiece resembling that of a European **TRUMPET** or French **HORN**, but smaller.

Because the mouthpiece is of an irregular bore, the harmonics obtained when playing the instrument can vary: Rather than a pure perfect fifth, intervals as narrow as a fourth, or as wide as a sixth may be produced.

The sounds

The two basic sounds of the **SHOFAR** are known as tekiah and teruah. They are of relatively low and high pitch, respectively. The tekiah is a plain deep blast ending abruptly; the teruah, a trill between two tekiahs. These sounds, constituting a bar of music, were rendered three times: First in honor of **God**'s kingship, next to recall the Binding of Isaac, and a third time to comply with the law regarding the **SHOFAR**. A third sound, the shevarim is a tekiah broken into three one-second segments. The duration of the teruah is equal to that of the shevarim; and the tekiah is half the length of either.

Ten appropriate verses from the Bible are recited at each repetition, which ends with a benediction. Over time doubts arose as to the correct sound of the teruah. The Talmud is uncertain as to whether it means a moaning or a staccato beat sound.

The sequence of the **SHOFAR** blowing is thus: Tekiah, shevarim-teruah, tekiah; tekiah, shevarim, tekiah; tekiah, teruah, and then a final blast of tekiah gadola which means "big tekiah," held as long as possible. This formula is repeated twice more, making 30 sounds for the series, with tekiah being one note, shevarium three, and teruah nine. This series of 30 sounds is repeated twice more, making 90 sounds in all. In addition to these three repetitions, a single formula of ten sounds is rendered at the close of the service, making a total of 100 sounds. According to the Sephardic tradition, a full 101 blasts are sounded, corresponding to the 100 cries of the mother of Sisera, the Cannanite general who did not make it home after being assassinated by the biblical heroine Yael (Judges 5:28). One cry is left to symbolize the legitimate love of a mother mourning her son.

The performer

A ba'al tekia

The expert who blows (or "blasts" or "sounds") the **SHOFAR** is termed the tokea (lit. "Blaster") or ba'al tekia (lit. "**Master** of the Blast"). Qualifications include someone who is learned in Torah and **God**-fearing. Every male Jew is eligible for this sacred office, providing he is acceptable to the congregation. If a potential choice will cause dissension, he should withdraw his candidacy, even if the improper person is chosen. In non-Orthodox congregations, females may also be eligible.

(From the Internet)

Spirit fell on the Youth

After I was done speaking at a special revival service for another organization, an older gentleman approached me. He told me that he was not Pentecostal, but he had appreciated my message. He said that he was in charge of the youth gathering Of the Church of **God**. This was the non-Pentecostal Church of **God** that he was referring to.

He said every year the regional district had a large gathering of the youth from the surrounding churches. Last year's meeting brought about 300 youth out. He asked if I might be interested in speaking at this meeting. He said the only thing is that I would not be able to minister on the subject of speaking in tongues.

I told him that I had no problem with this whatsoever. I said there are so many other things that **God** has done in my life, that there was plenty to share. He was basically interested in seeing the youth make a fresh commitment to wholeheartedly serving **Jesus**. I told him this was right up my alley. I love to preach on being sold out lock, stock, and barrel to **Jesus** and giving him every part of our life.

I asked him how it went with the meeting the previous year. He said that's one reason why he was asking me to speak because after hearing my message, a great conviction had hit him. He informed me that the year before when the speaker gave the altar call for re-commitment to Christ that out of almost 300 youth, only 2 to 3 youth responded.

*Because I'm a man under **God**'s authority, I always try to submit to the authority of the leadership of where I'm going to speak. If what they ask of me, is something that I believe would be displeasing to **God**, I just simply turned down the meeting. When I speak for people I ask them, how long do you want me to speak for? If they say 15 minutes, that is how long I speak. Can I give an altar call? Is there anything you do not want me to do? Based upon their response, and what they tell me, determines whether or not I perceive if I can accept or reject the offer.

In this particular situation, I had a great witness in my heart. I agreed to the place and the date that I was supposed to speak. About a week before this meeting was to take place; this gentleman called me very distraught. He told me that the pastors who send their youth found out that I was Pentecostal. That they were not going to be sending their youth that year. He said they were still going to have this meeting, but it would just be a small handful of young people. He asked me if I was okay with that.

I told him, absolutely I am okay with this. Let **God**'s will be done. I will praise the Lord for anyone who comes. The meeting time came, and I sat in the back, praying softly as approximately 30 young people were singing along with the song leader.

The time came for me to share my message. I gave them my testimony of my background, lifestyle, and struggles I had gone through as a youth. Then I shared the glorious, wonderful salvation I experienced on my 19th birthday. I began to preach a strong message that even as **Jesus** gave his all, so we should give our all. When I was done speaking, I gave them an opportunity for them to come forward, and to make a fresh commitment to Christ.

The previous year I was told that only three youth approximately out of 300 responded to the call. As I gave this challenge to the youth and opened up the alter EVERY ONE of those young people immediately came running to the front. The director who had asked me to come stood there with amazement on his face. The youth were crying out to **Jesus** and weeping with all of their hearts. The Holy Ghost had moved upon them in a wonderful and supernatural way.

Going Deeper in God

We were preparing to leave the church that we had been pastoring for two years. Because the church was bringing in new candidates for examination, they did not need me to preach the Word to them any longer.

As a result, I was able to spend many hours memorizing and meditating on the Bible. A sense of great expectancy grew within my heart. The air was charged with the tangible power of **God**. I would walk the mountain behind our parsonage praying and meditating all day long. This continued for a number of weeks. At the time, I did not realize that I was about to step into a deeper realm of the **Spirit**.

Mifflin FGBMFI Holy Ghost Meeting

My wife and I were scheduled to minister at a number of meetings, and I had been invited previously to minister at the Mifflin Full Gospel Businessmen's meeting located in Belleville, Pennsylvania. We arrived right before the meeting was to start.

As I sat at a table with my wife, I remember that I felt no particular quickening of the **Spirit** of **God** on the inside whatsoever. One of the members of the organization came over and asked me if I would like to pray with some of the members before the beginning of the meeting. I consented to do so.

They were standing in a circle holding each other's hands. I simply stepped into this circle and took the hand of the man on my right and left.

The Cataracts Just Melted Away

The men began to pray, and I prayed very softly, agreeing with them. During this time of prayer, I did not perceive in my heart that I should pray aloud. When we were done praying, the man on my right, an older gentleman, stared at me. He said, "What in the world was that?"

I said to him, **"What do you mean?"**

He said it was like a **streak of lightning** came out of my hand, and up to his arm, through his face. You could tell that something radical had taken place. I told him that I had not felt anything.

That was the beginning of a wonderful, strange, and unusual night. This same gentleman came to me at the end of the service, crying. He asked me to look into his eyes. I still remember to this day, his eyes were clear, glistening, and filled with tears. He said to me, **"My eyes were covered in cataracts. The minute you touched me, cataracts literally melted right off of my eyeballs!"** Thank you, **Jesus**!

Right up to the minute before I opened my mouth, I had not felt a single thing **Spirit**ually. However, the minute I began to speak at the pulpit, the river began to flow. I do not remember what I said, but I do know I was speaking under a strong influence of the Holy Ghost. Then I flowed right into the gifts of the **Spirit** after the teaching of the Word. A very precise word of knowledge began to operate. I remember looking out over the people and beginning to call specific people out. Many of the women and men appeared to be Mennonite or Amish.

I began to point to specific people and call them to come forward. As they came, I would tell them what it was that was going on in their bodies. When they would get within ten feet of me, (no exaggeration) they did not fall forward or backward, but just begin to crumple like soft snow flakes to the floor. Up to that time, I had never seen anything like it!

It was like they just simply, and very gently went down. As far as I know, all of them were instantly healed. I do not remember laying hands on anyone that night. The **Father**, Son, and Holy Ghost were in the house.

How God anointed Jesus of Nazareth with the Holy Ghost and with power: who went about doing good and healing all that were oppressed of the devil; for God was with him (Acts 10:38).

Her Face Hit the Concrete

We were conducting special healing meetings in Huntington, Pennsylvania, where we had rented a large conference room at Juniata College. The meeting room had a concrete floor with no carpet. After I had ministered the message, I began to move in the gifts of the **Spirit**.

In this particular meeting, I was quickened by the **Spirit** to have everyone stand facing the front in a long line. Quite a number of people had either been called out or wanted prayer. I specifically told the men that were standing behind these people not to brush against anyone's back. The reality of the presence of Christ was very strong. I knew that if someone brushed against these people, they would fall.

One of my coworkers accidentally brushed up against a young lady of approximately eighteen years of age. I was probably twenty feet from her. I saw the whole thing in slow motion. She began to fall forward. I went to move toward her, but I knew I could never make it in time. She fell forward with her hands at her side. I watched as her precious face slammed into the concrete floor. The minute her face hit the floor, it literally sounded like a pumpkin smashing and breaking in half, and everybody gasped in horror.

I walked up to where she was laying. Even though I had been in the **Spirit**, my flesh was filled with trembling. I was fully expecting there to be blood. As I looked around her head, I did not see any blood! I knew I had to quickly step back into the **Spirit**. As I did, I had total peace, so I left her lying there. I started at the end of the prayer line, working my way down, one person at a time. We saw many wonderful things that night. **God** set many free.

After the service, I looked for this young lady. She was standing about where she had originally fallen. I walked up to her very gingerly. I almost did not want to look at her face because I was afraid of what I would see. She was shaking a little and crying. When I came around to her front, I looked at her face.

To my amazement, there was not one mark. In the natural,

there had to be some damage. We all heard her head when it hit the concrete. The room was filled with the sound of a loud thump. But here she was with not one mark on her face. I asked her what happened when she fell forward. She said that when she hit the floor, it felt like as if she was falling into a bed of feathers!

A Divine Download of Revelation

Most times in our life as believers and ministers, we are trying to believe **God** for more power, more authority, and greater manifestations. In the life of Christ, it was the opposite. There was so much power, authority; **Spirit** manifested in his life; he knew everything he said would happen.

When you begin to walk in this realm is very important that you tiptoe. There have been several times in my life when I had tapped into this realm. What I said came to pass, whether I wanted to or not. Honestly! Let me share one such experience.

My wife and I were invited to minister at a woman's meeting in State College, Pennsylvania. On the way to this meeting, **God** began to supernaturally give me a message for this service. I have written over seven thousand sermon outlines through the years. Many of my sermons have come to me in dreams and visions. Numerous times I had simply preached what I saw myself speaking the night before from a dream I had received. All of these experiences are simply the quickening of the **Spirit**. We are all called as **God**'s people to walk in His quickening.

The first Adam was a living soul; the second Adam is a quickening **Spirit**. In this experience, I saw a multifaceted diamond that filled the heavens. Remember, this all took place as I was driving. I was in two different places at once.

I was driving my car with my wife next to me, and at the same time, I was in another world. As I looked at this multifaceted diamond, every one of its facets was a marvelous dimension of **God**'s nature and character. I was overwhelmed with **God**'s awesomeness and marvelous, never-ending possibilities. I wish someone would have recorded that sermon that day as it just flowed forth from heaven through me.

They Were Hit with an Invisible Bowling Ball

When I had finished ministering the Word of **God** at this woman's meeting, I began to operate in a precise word of knowledge. (1981)

As I spoke forth what the **Spirit** of **God** showed me by a word of knowledge, I asked all the ladies that I had spoken to by the **Spirit** of the Lord to step out into the center of the room. The atmosphere was **electrified by the Power of God** to heal the sick. Approximately fifteen to twenty women (maybe more) were standing in the middle of the room waiting to be ministered to. The **Spirit** of **God** told me specifically:

"Do Not Touch Them. Simply Speak My Word."

I heard this very strong within my inner man, and oh, how I wish I had listened to the **Voice** of **God**. Now, there was one woman who was standing in front of all the rest. They were lined up in such a way that it looked almost like bowling pins set up at the end of a bowling alley.

At that moment, un-crucified flesh rose up in me, and I disobeyed **God**. I was not just going to speak to them, but I would lay my hands on each one, and they would be healed, and wouldn't I be something (Me, Me, Me)! That's why **God** cannot use a lot of people —because they start thinking that they are something special. I reached out Oh so very gently touching the very first woman on the forehead with just the tip of my fingers. My wife was there, and she can testify to this story.

The minute I touched this precious lady, she flew back violently. She was literally thrown back as if a mighty power had struck her. She hit the ladies right behind her. Every one of these ladies flew back like the first lady and slammed into the others. They all fail violently to the floor.

These precious ladies ended up on the floor, lying on top of one another in less than three seconds. There were exposed legs sticking up in the air everywhere. I am ashamed to say that even some of their dresses were lifted above their waist with their undergarments exposed. When they all flew back, it looked like a bowling ball slamming into the bowling pins as a strike.

At that very moment, the **Spirit** of **God** spoke to me and said: because of your disobedience, not one of them had been healed. If I had obeyed **God**, every one of them would have been instantly delivered and healed. Now, instead of **God** being glorified, confusion had entered this meeting. I had misused and abused my position with **God**. To this day, I am ashamed that I didn't obey **God** that night. Just think if I would have listened to the Lord; those precious ladies would have all been healed instantly, and **God** would have been glorified. I did apologize to those present.

My wife and I helped the ladies get back up, and I told them I would like to pray for each one of them individually because they testified that none of them were healed. When you don't obey, there is a price to pay. Many ministers I think simply use the power of **God** to knock people down. But by faith, you need to direct that power of the **Spirit** into their bodies to heal them. Kathleen and I prayed for each person, but this time, it was with what the Bible calls "common faith" while before I had been operating in the gift of faith and healing.

(2 Samuel 24:10) And David's heart smote him after that he had numbered the people. And David said unto the LORD, I have sinned greatly in that I have done: and now, I beseech thee, O LORD, take away the iniquity of thy servant; for I have done very foolishly.

CHAPTER TEN

How to See a Move of GOD

FIRST CHRIST MUST BE EXALTED!

All of our life as a believer is based on the revelation of **JESUS CHRIST**. From Matthew chapter 1 to the end of the book of Revelation, **JESUS CHRIST** is spoken of in a personal way over 9000 times. It is at the revelation of **JESUS CHRIST** in which faith will begin to arise in your heart to accomplish the perfect will of the **FATHER**.

Without this revelation of who **CHRIST** is, we can accomplish nothing. Go over these Scriptures slowly as you meditate upon them, asking the **Holy Spirit** to quicken them to you in a profound way, in order to transform you into the likeness and the image of **God**. In order to become a partaker of all of **God**'s wonderful nature and **Divine** characteristics.

I believe that every human being hears the **VOICE** of **God**; they simply do not respond to him. They hardened their hearts to the **VOICE** of **God** because of the carnal flesh wars against the **Spirit**, and the **Spirit** against the flesh. When a man committed sin in the garden, the seed of lust entered into the flesh and heart of man, the DNA of Satan. Before man committed sin he responded instantly to the **VOICE** of **God**, but Adam and his wife partook of the forbidden fruit, and now instead of running to **God** at the sound of his **VOICE**, they found themselves running from him. They became slaves to the dictates of the desires and lust of the sin in their flesh.

Genesis 3:8 And they heard the VOICE of the Lord God walking in the garden in the cool of the day: and Adam and his wife hid themselves from the presence of the Lord God amongst the trees of the garden.

There is the **VOICE** of the **Spirit** and the **VOICE** of the flesh, and you have to know which **VOICE** it is that is speaking to you. Granted sometimes it gets a little bit difficult and challenging to determine which **VOICE** is speaking to us. The very first thing we need to do is to build a solid foundation by which we can determine if what we're hearing is the **VOICE** of **God**'s **Spirit** or the **VOICE** of our flesh.

In this first chapter, I would like to share with you the two main ways that **God** speaks to His people. You need to read this first chapter over and over, unto you truly understand these two major ways that **God** leads and guides us. It may seem like these two ways are the same, but believe me when I say: that they are not.

For this particular chapter, I will be using ***Hebrews chapter 1***, and the gospel of ***John chapter 1***. These two chapters will help build an amazing foundation for hearing the **VOICE** of **God**, and with **Spirit**ual discernment, for every situation. If you embrace what is revealed in these two chapters, your understanding will be greatly enlightened. Let us now take a look at Hebrews chapter 1.

Hebrews **1:1 God, who at sundry times and in divers manners spake in time past unto the FATHERs by the prophets, 2 hath in these last days spoken unto us by his Son, whom he hath appointed heir of all things, by whom also he made the worlds; 3 who being the brightness of his glory, and the express image of his person, and upholding all things by the word of his power, when he had by himself purged our sins, sat down on the right hand of the Majesty on high;**

In Hebrews 1, it is revealed that **God** had spoken to the **FATHER**s by the prophets but has now spoken to us by his Son **JESUS CHRIST**. According to ***Ephesians chapter 2:20, the kingdom of God is built upon the apostles and prophets, JESUS CHRIST himself being the chief cornerstone.*** Please notice that in times past **God** spoke specifically by the prophets to the **FATHER**'s, now we have a more sure word of prophecy, a deeper revelation, a more precise understanding of the perfect will of our heavenly **FATHER**.

Why? Because he's going to speak to us in a very clear and

dramatic way. If we believe the words, the life, and the example of **JESUS**, it will radically transform our lives forever. Remember all the words that had been spoken up to the coming of **CHRIST** were to prepare us for the coming of **CHRIST**. The life of **JESUS** is the perfect will of **God** manifested in the flesh.

This is the mystery which had been hidden before the foundation of the world. Notice Hebrews 1: in verse 2 ***hath in these last days spoken unto us by his Son!*** The foundation of my understanding of the **VOICE** of **God**, the will of **God**, the purposes of **God**, the plan of **God**, the mission of **God**, the mysteries of **God** cannot be discovered in any greater revelation than the person of **JESUS CHRIST**! **There is no greater revelation of God's perfect Divine will or VOICE then that we discover in JESUS CHRIST.** I cannot emphasize this enough!

John 1:14 And the Word was made flesh, and dwelt among us, (and we beheld his glory, the glory as of the only begotten of the FATHER,) full of grace and truth.

If you do not understand that **God** is speaking to you very precisely through his son **JESUS CHRIST**, you will end up being mixed up, confused, and led astray. Learning to hear the **VOICE** of **God** very precisely is only found in **JESUS CHRIST**, whom he has appointed heir of all things, by whom also he made the worlds. Notice Hebrews Chapter 1 Verse 3 boldly declares that **JESUS CHRIST** is the brightness of the **FATHER**'s glory, the manifestation of the **FATHER**'s presence, and the express image of His personality. He is like a mirror reflecting the perfect image of the heavenly **FATHER** to all of humanity. **JESUS** declared:

John 14:9 JESUS saith unto him, have I been so long time with

you, and yet hast thou not known me, Philip? He that hath seen me hath seen the FATHER; and how sayest thou then, Shew us the FATHER? 10 Believest thou not that I am in the FATHER, and the FATHER in me? The words that I speak unto you I speak not of myself: but the FATHER that dwelleth in me, he doeth the works.

JESUS CHRIST is the absolute perfect will of the **FATHER** revealed to you and me. The deepest revelation of the **FATHER** is only discovered in **JESUS CHRIST**! Paul, the apostle, commands us to have the mind of **CHRIST**.

Philippians 2:5 Let this mind be in you, which was also in CHRIST JESUS: 6 who, being in the form of God, thought it not robbery to be equal with God: 7 but made himself of no reputation, and took upon him the form of a servant, and was made in the likeness of men: 8 and being found in fashion as a man, he humbled himself, and became obedient unto death, even the death of the cross. 9 Wherefore God also hath highly exalted him, and given him a name which is above every name: 10 that at the name of JESUS every knee should bow, of things in heaven, and things in earth, and things under the earth; 11 and that every tongue should confess that JESUS CHRIST is Lord, to the glory of God the FATHER.

When we look at **JESUS** and hear His words, it is the **FATHER** we are looking at! The apostle John boldly declares this in John 1.

John 1:1 In the beginning was the Word, and the Word was with God, and the Word was God. 2 The same was in the beginning with God. 3 All things were made by him; and without him was not anything made that was made.

All things were made by the word. What word is it talking about in these scriptures? Is it talking about the written word or **CHRIST** the word? It is obvious that it is talking about the person **CHRIST JESUS**, Emmanuel **God** with us!

John 1:14 And the Word was made flesh, and dwelt among us, (and we beheld his glory, the glory as of the only begotten of the FATHER,) full of grace and truth.

The reality is that we have to know the person of **CHRIST** discovered in the four Gospels for us to rightly discern the Word of **God**. What do I mean by this statement? When I gave my heart to **JESUS CHRIST** on February 18, 1975, at about 3 PM in the afternoon, all I had available was a little military green Bible. At the moment **CHRIST** came into my heart, I picked up that little Bible and began to devour it. Matthew, Mark, Luke, and John, the 4 Gospels of **JESUS CHRIST** became my favorite books.

I just could not get enough of the wonderful reality of **JESUS**. As I read these 4 Gospels, I walked with **CHRIST** every step of the way. From his birth, through his childhood, his baptism by John when he was 30 years old. When he was baptized by the **Holy** Ghost, and he was led of the **Spirit** into the wilderness, tempted of the enemy overcoming by boldly declaring, "It is written."

I spent my first three years as a believer eating and drinking nothing but **JESUS** from the four Gospels. Yes, I did read the epistles, and they were wonderful, but nothing captured and captivated my heart as much as the life, the words and the ministry of **JESUS CHRIST**. I wept as I read of his sufferings, his crucifixion, and his death. I wept when I saw that the Heavenly **FATHER** had to turn his face away from his own Son, because of his love for us. I shouted at the triumphant conquest and victory that **JESUS** had over every satanic power.

JESUS CHRIST is the perfect reflection of the Heavenly **FATHER**. There is no more perfect revelation of the will of the **FATHER** than **JESUS CHRIST**. I am extremely happy that I was not influenced by the modern day church for the first three years of my salvation. When I eventually came to the lower 48, after living and ministering in Alaska, I was shocked and surprised at what most **Christ**ians believed. I did not realize that there was such a large variety of different interpretation of the Scriptures in the churches. Many of **God**'s people are extremely confused.

Many ministers declare insane false doctrines that are so contrary to what I discovered in **CHRIST**; it is hard for me to believe that they even believe what they're teaching. To truly know the **VOICE** of **God**, all you have to do is look at **JESUS CHRIST**: His words, deeds, actions, and reactions; His lifestyle and his attitude, mannerism, wonderful character, and the fruit of his life. I can truly say that since I have been born again, I have only had one person who I truly want to be like: His name is **JESUS CHRIST**.

If the body of **CHRIST** would simply go back to the 4 Gospels, and walk with **JESUS** every step of the way, from his birth to his resurrection, to his ascension, much of their confusion would be gone. I believe the reason why so many believers are being deceived by false doctrines and philosophies in America today is that they do not know or understand **JESUS CHRIST**.

Hebrews 13:8, "JESUS CHRIST the same yesterday, and today, and forever."

In the old covenant, **God** says, **"I am the Lord, and I**

change not." Without truly seeing the **FATHER** through the words, the ministry and the life of **JESUS CHRIST,** you can easily be led astray by crafty men misusing Scriptures. You have to see **JESUS** to understand not just the Old Testament but also the epistles of the New Testament. **JESUS** is the **VOICE** of **God**, the absolute perfect will of the **FATHER**.

I have heard ministers use the Bible to contradict the teachings of **JESUS CHRIST**. The reason why false doctrines have been able to take root in the church is that people have not looked and listened to **Jesus** in the four Gospels. If in your mind and heart you will exalt **Christ**, and his teaching above all else, will be very difficult for the enemy to lead you astray with false teachings and doctrines. Here is an example when it comes to the will of **God** about **Divine** healing.

About three days later, I was contacted by one of the daughters of William. They were extremely excited because her father had made a complete and absolute recovery. His eyesight had come back, and his brain, mental awareness had completely returned. That Thanksgiving he was home eating turkey with the rest of the family. To the writing of this book, he is still doing wonderfully. Every day his children walk with him down the paths and the roads of the forest they live in, right outside of Chambersburg Pennsylvania. **God** still answers prayer when we pray in faith, believing.

<u>SECOND</u> WE MUST EMBRACE GODS WORD

The Written Word, the Bible equals the audible **VOICE** of **God**. This is the **VOICE** of **God**, and it must become more real to you than anything else in this world. Believers tell me all the time that **God** does not speak to them, but they are sadly mistaken. He speaks to us through the **Holy** book called the Bible.

2 Timothy 3:16 All scripture is given by inspiration of God and is profitable for doctrine, for reproof, for correction, for instruction in righteousness:

God speaks to us is through the written word. Remember that **CHRIST**, His Life and His words are the 1st major way and foundation that we must build upon for hearing the **VOICE** of **God**! Only when this truth is established in my heart, can I go to all of the written word, the epistles, and the Old Testament with understanding. What must take priority over all Scripture is what **JESUS** said and did?

After this reality, then I can go to the epistles of Paul, Peter, Philip, James, the book of Jude, and all of the WORD with **Divine** and clear understanding. For example, some people are still teaching and promoting physical circumcision, **Holy** days, feast days, Sabbath days, new Moon days because they do not know that **JESUS CHRIST** is the embodiment of all of these **Levitical** laws.

Colossians 2:16 Let no man, therefore, judge you in meat, or in drink, or in respect of an Holyday, or of the new moon, or of the sabbath days: 17 which are a shadow of things to come; but the body is of CHRIST.

Many of the Old Testament miracles were types and shadows of **JESUS CHRIST**. The Passover Lamb, manna from heaven, water from the rock, the snake on the brazen pole. **JESUS CHRIST** is the will and the **VOICE** of **God** speaking loud and clear to the human race. Now with this reality, the pure Word of **God** can work mightily within our lives.

Hebrews 4:12 For the word of God is quick, and powerful, and sharper than any two-edged sword, piercing even to the dividing asunder of soul and Spirit, and of the joints and marrow, and is a discerner of the thoughts and intents of the heart.

1 Peter 2:2 as newborn babes, desire the sincere milk of the word, that ye may grow thereby:

1 Peter 1:23 being born again, not of corruptible seed, but of incorruptible, by the word of God, which liveth and abideth forever.

The very 1st reality that will build an unmovable foundation in our hearts is the life of **JESUS**, the works of **JESUS**, the words of **JESUS**, the attitude of **JESUS,** and the conduct of **JESUS**! David declared that he hid the word of **God** in his heart so that he would not sin against **God**. The apostle Paul shared this amazing revelation in Romans chapter 12.

Romans 12:2 And be not conformed to this world: but be ye transformed by the renewing of your mind, that ye may prove what is that good, and acceptable, and perfect, will of God.

Remember that **JESUS** in John 17 is no longer speaking to his disciples, but is speaking directly to his heavenly **FATHER**. He reveals some amazing realities and **Spirit**ual insights into how we are to become one with Him, the heavenly **FATHER**, and the **Holy** Ghost.

John 17:17 Sanctify them through thy truth: thy word isthe truth.

John 17:19 And for their sakes I sanctify myself, that they also might be sanctified through the truth.

In Ephesians, the apostle Paul tells us that husbands are to love their wives as **CHRIST** also loved the church. That **CHRIST** gave himself for the church so that he might sanctify and cleanse it with the washing of the water of the word. That he might present to himself a glorious church, without spot or wrinkle or any such thing, let me challenge you with a bold statement: **CHRIST** is the audible, visible manifested **VOICE** of the **FATHER** sent to the earth in human flesh! All of the other Scriptures from Genesis to Revelation simply verify who **JESUS** is, what he accomplished, what **JESUS** taught, and did!

2 Timothy 3:16 All scripture is given by inspiration of God and is profitable for doctrine, for reproof, for correction, for instruction in righteousness: 17 that the man of God may be perfect, thoroughly furnished unto all good works.

We have a look at the word through the person of **JESUS CHRIST**. We will never really understand the word of **God**, or the will of **God** without looking at it through our Lord **JESUS CHRIST**. Many Ministers are wrongly emphasizing on finances, materialism, and many other subjects because they do not know **JESUS CHRIST**, or what is important to him and his **FATHER**! Ministers are constantly emphasizing the anointing when they should be emphasizing the reality of **JESUS CHRIST**.

Many are not even preaching and teaching about **JESUS** in the pulpit today the way they should because they're not looking at the word of **God** through **CHRIST**. He is the way, the truth, and the light. No man comes to the **FATHER** but by **JESUS CHRIST**. There is no other name under heaven given among men whereby we must be saved. I understand the **FATHER** through

JESUS CHRIST. I understand the Bible through **JESUS CHRIST**. Because of **JESUS CHRIST**, the word of **God** is more real to me than my natural physical circumstances. Let me share with you one of the amazing experiences that I have had because of this revelation I have in **CHRIST** and his eternal word.

Meditation of the Word

If you study the context of Romans chapter 10, it is talking about the preaching of **JESUS CHRIST**! When ministers preach **JESUS CHRIST** out of a heart filled with faith, that faith is **contagious**. This is when the Power of **God** will fall! That's why we need to preach **JESUS CHRIST** because it is all about **JESUS**, through him, to him, and by him. This is why in the New Testament from Matthew to the end of the book of Revelation about 163 pages, 7,957 Scriptures, **JESUS CHRIST** himself is referred to in a personal, intimate way over 9000 times!

At this moment we are living in an actual physical world, with our feet on the ground. This planet we are on is spinning around the sun, the moon is spinning around the earth, and we have Jupiter, Mars, and Venus, all these other planets spinning around the sun. Now we call this invisible power gravitation. Gravitation is an amazing invisible force that scientists still do not fully understand. Scripture declares that **God upholds all things by the power of His Power.** I believe the invisible force we call gravitation is **God's faith** manifested. In the New Testament, you can go to any chapter, and discover the subject of faith! Why because it's all about faith in **JESUS CHRIST!**

Acts 17:28 For in him we live, and move, and have our being; as certain also of your own poets have said, For we are also his offspring.

In the book of Romans chapter 12, we will see the **third way in which faith comes**, but first, I need to give you a word of warning. Let's look in Romans, chapter 14.

Romans 14:22 Hast thou faith? Have it to thyself before God. Happy is he that condemneth, not himself in that thing which he alloweth.

Your faith in **God** is not dependent upon any other person. You can go as high and deep to **God** by faith as you want. **Romans** chapter **14:22** is a warning, in which it is talking about the Sabbath days, **Holy** days, meats. It is talking about the convictions of what people perceive to be the will of **God**. Now here is the danger, you can have convictions about what you believe to be the will of **God** when it is not his will, but now you will have to live under these convictions because anything that is not of faith is a sin.

1 Timothy 4:3-5 forbidding to marry, and commanding to abstain from meats, which God hath created to be received with thanksgiving of them which believe and know the truth. 4 For every creature of God is good, and nothing to be refused, if it is received with thanksgiving: 5 for it is sanctified by the word of God and prayer.

There are many **Christ**ians who are weak in their faith. Who is weak in the faith but people who take to themselves convictions that do not make a difference? They get caught up in all kind of crusades dealing with meats, **Holy** days, Sabbath days, clothing when it's all about the character, nature, and **Divine** attributes of

God.

Romans 14:1-3 Him that is weak in the faith receive ye, but not to doubtful disputations. 2 For one believeth that he may eat all things: another, who is weak, eateth herbs. 3 Let not him that eateth despise him that eateth not; and let not him which eateth not judge him that eateth: for God hath received him. To verse :5 One man esteemeth one day above another: another esteemeth every day alike. Let every man be fully persuaded in his own mind. 6 He that regardeth the day, regardeth it unto the Lord; and he that regardeth not the day, to the Lord he doth not regard it.

The perfect will of **God** is revealed to us through **JESUS CHRIST**. He is the brightness of **God**'s glory, the express image of his person. If you have seen **JESUS CHRIST**, then you have seen the **FATHER**. Let us now adventure into the **third way in which faith comes**.

Romans 12:12 I beseech you therefore, brethren, by the mercies of God, that ye present your bodies a living sacrifice, Holy, acceptable unto God, which is your reasonable service. 2 And be not conformed to this world: but be ye transformed by the renewing of your mind, that ye may prove what is that good, and acceptable, and perfect, will of God. What is that good, and acceptable, and perfect, will of God.

The third important reality is the renewing of our mind by meditating on Scriptures! There must be a transformation in our thinking processes by the means of meditation. You have to take your head and your heart and give them to **God**. I mean all of who you are, needs to be given to **God**.

Isaiah 26:3 Thou wilt keep him in perfect peace, whose mind is

stayed on thee: because he trusteth in thee.

Proverbs 3:5 Trust in the LORD with all thine heart; and lean not unto thine own understanding.6 In all thy ways acknowledge him, and he shall direct thy paths.

The Scriptures declare that if **two be not agreed together, they cannot walk together**. Faith is when you come into complete agreement with **God**, his Word, and his will. Paul said by the **Spirit** of **God**, be not conformed to this world, but be ye transformed (**metamorphosis**) this means being changed by the renewing of our mind.

Before your mind is transformed, renewed we are like a **caterpillar**. The number of legs and feet that a **caterpillar** has varied. There is one type of caterpillar that has 16 legs, and 16 feet, which they use to hold on to anything, and everything they can. When that **caterpillar** becomes a **Butterfly**, everything changes. Including the number of feet they have, and their purpose. All Butterflies end up with SIX legs and feet. In some species such as the monarch, the front pair of legs remains tucked up under the body most of the time. Their legs become long and slender, and something amazing happens to their feet because within their feet are now taste buds.

That means that whatever their feet touch they taste. It prevents them from eating anything that is not good for them. When they were **caterpillars,** they were willing to eat everything their little feet took a hold of. You see the **Butterfly,** which came from the caterpillar now lives in a completely different world. It is no longer bound by earthly things. It no longer has feet that cling to the Earth! It is free to fly above all the worries, fears, anxieties, enemies, and circumstances of life.

It literally can see into the future, where it is going. It has overcome the law of gravitation, by a superior law. It is called the law of aerodynamics. We as believers, as we renew our minds leave behind the law of sin and death, entering into a new world called: **The Law of the Spirit of Life in CHRIST JESUS**! We need to be very picky about what we eat mentally. Whatever we place in our minds and our hearts, is what we will meditate upon. As **a man thinketh, so is he!**

Romans 8:2 For the law of the Spirit of life in CHRIST JESUS hath made me free from the law of sin and death.

To operate in **God**'s kingdom, you need to **renew your mind**. Your faith level cannot be higher than that of the **renewing of your mind**. Everything that is contradictory to the word, the will, the **Divine** nature of **JESUS CHRIST** must be dealt with. As we bring every thought captive to the obedience of **CHRIST**, our faith will soar like an eagle. Listen to what James the brother of **JESUS** said about the renewing of the mind.

James 1:21Wherefore lay apart all filthiness and superfluity of naughtiness, and receive with meekness the engrafted word, which is able to save your souls.

WE CAN NOT BE DEFEATED WHEN LIVING, WALKING & MOVING IN FAITH!

What if I told you that your usefulness to God can only equal the level of faith you have in CHRIST! The faith I am referring to is true faith. This is a faith that will take a hold of God (like Jacob wrestling with the Angel) refusing to let go until there is a wonderful transformation in your Heart and your Mind!

There are so many Scriptures dealing with the renewing of your mind, and the meditation of your heart, that many books could easily be written on this subject. I will share with you only a small number of Scriptures that are important to this particular chapter. Then I will share with you how you meditate.

Joshua 1:8 This book of the law shall not depart out of thy mouth; but thou shalt meditate therein day and night, which thou mayest observe to do according to all that is written therein: for then thou shalt make thy way prosperous, and then thou shalt have good success.

Psalm 1:2 But his delight is in the law of the Lord; and in his law doth he meditate day and night.

Psalm 63:6 when I remember thee upon my bed, and meditate on thee in the night watches.

Psalm 77:12 I will meditate also of all thy work, and talk of thy doings.

Psalm 119:148 Mine eyes prevent the night watches, that I might meditate in thy word.

Psalm 104:34 My meditation of him shall be sweet: I will be glad in the Lord.

Psalm 119:97 O how love I thy law! it is my meditation all the day.

Psalm 119:99 I have more understanding than all my teachers: for thy testimonies are my meditation.

Timothy 4:15 Meditate upon these things; give thyself wholly to them; that thy profiting may appear to all.

Psalm 39:3 My heart was hot within me, while I was musing the FIRE burned: then spake I with my tongue,

Samuel 23:2 The Spirit of the Lord spake by me, and his word was in my tongue.

What Is Meditation?

To meditate means to Muse, to ponder, to think Upon, To Mutter, Recite, To Talk to Yourself. It is way more than just memorization. In the most basic form, it would be what we call to worry, but it's the opposite of worry. When you worry about something, it is like a record stuck in a groove that keeps playing over and over. Have you ever had a song that just would not leave your mind? You sang it to yourself in your mind, and even with your lips because it got into your head and your heart. This is what meditation is. We need to meditate upon the word, the will, the personality of **JESUS CHRIST** day and night. This will bring about a wonderful transformation.

In nature, **God** has given us many examples that can be applied to **Spirit**ually. I think one of the greatest examples of meditation is revealed to us through the process of dairy cows, turning green grass into wonderful white and creamy milk.

How do Cows Make Milk?

Or we could say:

How do Believers Produce Faith?

#1 First A cow only starts to produce milk once her first calf is born.

(Even so, we must become impregnated by the Word of God, being born again by the Spirit and the water, in order to walk where JESUS walked)

#2 A cow will only produce milk for as long as she keeps eating massive amounts of living green grass, chewing the cud, and are milked. If any of these processes stop, she will stop producing milk.

(The believer must keep eating the living word of God, chewing it, and then doing it! Doing it would equal that of the dairy cow being milked!)

John 6:53 Then JESUS said unto them, Verily, verily, I say unto you, Except ye eat the flesh of the Son of man, and drink his blood, ye have no life in you. 54 Whoso eateth my flesh, and drinketh my blood, hath eternal life; and I will raise him up at the last day. 55 For my flesh is meat indeed, and my blood is drink indeed.

#3 Cows belong to a group of animals called ruminants. All of these animals have **four stomach compartments,** and each compartment has a specific part in digesting food. [Amazingly sheep are included in this animal group.] The transformation of grass into milk is not instantaneous or accomplished quickly. It will take about **70 hours** for a cow to turn green grass into milk!

(Even so is it with faith. As you begin to meditate upon the word consistently hour after hour, day after day, faith will

begin to be produced in your heart and your life! Many believers do not have this understanding. They chew a little bit of the word, for a little bit of time, and then are disappointed when faith dose not pour out of their hearts like a mighty river)

#4 Blood has a significant part of the cow producing milk. For every **2 to 3 cups of milk** a cow makes, more than **105 gallons** of blood must travel around her udder to deliver the nutrients and water for making milk. In total a cow has about **12 gallons** of blood in her body, so her blood is always **on the move** around the udder to keep making milk.

Even so with the believer, there must be continual moving of the Holy Spirit in our lives for us to produce faith. This is why JESUS asked: will there be any faith left on the earth when he returns? It is because there is very little moving of the Spirit in many church gatherings today, much less in a believer's everyday life. And yet in Ephesians it tells us to be filled with the Spirit beginning in chapter 5 verse 17. It will take massive amounts of the word and the moving of the Spirit to produce the faith that is necessary to live the same life that JESUS did!

#5 To produce milk, cows must eat a variety of grasses, clover and bulky fodder, which make them feel full, plus food rich in protein and energy. If the pasture (**pastor**) they are eating from is not providing the right kind of foods, it will cause the cow to produce dismal results. It only takes the cow to be eating one wrong type of vegetation for it to ruin its milk. And it can have dire consequences to the health of the cow. It could even die!

(Even so is it with the believer. If the pastor (pasture) is not providing healthy, Spiritual truths, preaching the reality of JESUS CHRIST, His will and His purposes, it will not produce faith that prevails and overcomes the obstacles of life)

Now let us look at the four stomach compartments (digestive compartments) and their unique functions:

The stomach: The heart of man, his mind, will, emotions, attitude, disposition, the purpose of living could be likened unto the cow's stomach.

1. The rumen

When cows graze on grass, they swallow the grass half-chewed and mix it with water in their first stomach - the rumen - which can hold about **13 gallons** of chewed grass. It is here that the digestive process begins. The rumen softens and breaks down the grass with stomach juices and microbes (or bacteria).

*(Even so with the believer, we begin to hide Scriptures within our heart. We memorize these Scriptures. This is the first process. The **Holy Spirit** can do very little with the Scriptures unto they are memorized)*

2. The reticulum

In the reticulum, the grass is made even softer and is formed into small wads called cuds. Each cud is then returned to the mouth where the cow chews it **40 to 60** times (for about one minute). Each card is chewed for almost an hour!

(After the believer has memorized the Scripture it now must be spoken (chewed) for at least an hour. Within this time fRAMe, the Holy Spirit begins to change the word of God from letter into the Spirit.)

3. The omasum

The chewed cud is swallowed into the third stomach, the omasum, where it is pressed to remove water and broken down further.

(This is where things begin to get interesting because now the word begins to be assimilated into your heart. It begins to take upon it a reality that you have never known. It begins to renew and transform your mind).

King David said: My heart was hot within me, while I was musing the FIRE burned: then spake I with my tongue,

4. The abomasum

The grass then passes to the fourth stomach, called the abomasum, where it is digested. The digested grass then passes through the small intestine, where all the essential nutrients the cow needs to stay healthy and strong are absorbed, and some are transported to the udder.

(Life is now beginning to flood the believer. Divine wisdom and strength are beginning to overtake him or her. The reality of CHRIST is exploding in their minds, their thoughts, their deeds, and their actions. Even as the milk comes forth from the utter of the cow, so now the works of the kingdom are being produced through our lives. People are beginning to see, hear, and experience JESUS CHRIST in and through us!)

Men, woman, children COULD NOT MOVE or SPEAK for 2 1/2 hours

My family and I traveled out West ministering in different churches and visiting relatives in Wisconsin. We were invited to speak at a church in Minneapolis, Minnesota. The pastor had two different churches that he pastored. One of these churches was in the suburbs, and the other one was in the heart of Minneapolis. The larger of the two churches was in the suburbs. I was to minister at the larger church first and then immediately go to his other church downtown. The whole congregation was in the same service that morning. There were approximately 140 to 160 people, including women, men, children, and babies in the sanctuary.

As I began to speak, I found myself unexpectedly speaking on the subject of the year that King Uzziah died, I saw the Lord high and lifted up, and his glory filled the Temple, which is found in the book of Isaiah! The unction of the **Holy** Ghost was upon me so strong that it just flowed out of my belly like rivers of living water. To this day, I do not remember everything that I said. As I was speaking, I sensed an amazing heavenly touch of **God**'s presence on myself and everyone in the sanctuary.

The **Spirit** of **God** was on me in a mighty way, and yet I was aware of the time factor. To get to Pastor Bill's sister church downtown Minnesota, I was not going to have time to lay hands on or pray for anyone. If **God** were going to confirm his word with signs following, then he would have to do it without me being there. It turns out that is exactly what **God** wanted to do!

When I was at the limit of the amount of time allotted to me, I quickly closed with a prayer. I did not say anything to the pastor or anyone else as I grabbed my Bible to leave the sanctuary. My family was already loaded up and waiting for me in our vehicle. As I ran out the door, I perceived something strange, awesome, and wonderful was beginning to happen to the congregation. There was a heavy, unusual, and **Holy** hush that had come upon them.

By the time I arrived at the other church; their worship had already begun. As I stood up in the pulpit to Minister **God**'s Word, the **Holy Spirit** began to speak to me again, with a completely, different message. **God** did wonderful things in the sister church downtown that afternoon as I preached a message on being radically sold out and committed to **CHRIST**.

Everyone ended up falling out of their chairs to the floor on their faces, weeping and crying before the Lord. This is not something I have ever encouraged any congregation to do. I have seen this happen numerous times where I simply must stop preaching because the presence of **God** is so strong, and so real that people cannot stay in their seats. I would stop preaching, get on my face, and just wait on **God**, as he moved on the people's hearts.

After that service, we went back to our fifth wheel trailer at the local campgrounds where we were camping. Later in the day, I received a phone call from this pastor. He was acting rather strange and speaking very softly in a very hushed manner.

He asked me with a whisper: does that always happen after you are done preaching? I said to him, tell me what happened. He said, "As you were headed out the door, I began to melt to the floor, I could not keep standing, and I found myself pinned to the floor of the sanctuary. I could not move or speak."

Now all the children (including babies) were in the sanctuary with the rest of the congregation. He said he could not move for two and a half hours. During this whole experience, he did not hear another sound in the facility. For over two and a half hours, he just simply laid there not being able to move or speak a word under the presence and mighty hand of **God**. After two and a half hours Pastor Bill was able to move finally and to get up.

He had thought for sure that he was the only one still left in the church. Everybody must have gone home a long time ago, and that he was there by himself. But to his complete shock and amazement, everybody was still there, laying on the floor. Nobody could move or speak for over two and a half hours! Men, women, children, and even the babies were still lying on the floor, not moving, talking, or crying! **God** was in the house! The tangible, overwhelming, solemn, presence, and **Holiness** of **God** had come!

Pastor Bill asked me to come over to his house so we could talk about what happened that day in his church service. My family and I arrived. He invited us inside. He asked if this normally happens wherever I went. I informed him, no, but many wonderful and strange things do take place. It did not always happen, except when I get myself in a place of complete, absolute surrender and submission to **JESUS CHRIST**.

This submission included not putting ANYTHING else but the WORD of **God** into my heart. When I simply seek the face of **God**, by praying, giving myself completely to the word, meditation, singing and worship, intimacy with the **FATHER**, Son, and **Holy** Ghost, this was the result! **God** is not a respecter of people; what he does for one; he will do for others!

God Moved Upon Rapist & Murderers!

My 2nd son Daniel and I went to minister in a little country called Suriname (this little nation's population is basically of African slavery descent). While we were there, we were invited to a men's high-security prison. They wanted us to speak to young men who had been incarcerated for the serious crimes of murder, rape, and terrible deeds. We agreed to do this. There was a **God**ly young mother who had a burden for these young boys. They were prisoners from 12 years old up to 18. She told us that she had seen very little results even though she had been pouring her life and much prayer into this endeavor. This day her prayers finally paid off.

My son Daniel was to be the one to minister to them because he was in his 20s. This precious lady felt that if they heard a young man speak, it might touch them. As my son spoke, he was sharing about his life, but it did not seem like it was having much of if any effect upon them whatsoever. He finally turned the service over to me.

I began to share my life experience, how **God** had delivered me from drugs, alcohol, violence, and running with a gang outside of Chicago. As I was speaking, I happen to look over at my son Daniel, and I saw and perceived that the **Spirit of God was moving upon him in a mighty way**. The hair on the back of my neck stood up, the **Spirit of the Lord was upon him so powerfully**. Intermediately I turned this meeting back over to him. A tremendous prophetic word began to come forth out of his mouth. I can tell you without any doubt, it was not my son speaking, but the **Spirit** of the living **God**.

He began to talk about a young man named Joseph, and how Joseph had ended up in prison wrongfully. While he was in prison, he had maintained a **Spirit** of integrity and love for **God**. Even in prison, he never became bitter, or angry at **God** or others.
He just kept pressing in and taking hold of the Lord no matter what his condition or situation was.

Because of Joseph's **God**ly disposition and seeking that the Lord had eventually put Joseph second in charge over all the land of Egypt (which was the most powerful nation in the world at the time) overnight. Daniel told them that no matter why they were there, or their present condition, that if they would truly cry out to **God** with all their hearts, turning their lives over to **JESUS CHRIST**, they could become a Joseph.

As my son preached underneath this heavy anointing, the **Spirit of God fell upon these young men**. I sat there in utter amazement as I watched an amazing transformation before all of our eyes as each and every one of them surrendered their lives to **JESUS CHRIST** on the spot! When my son was done, the **Spirit** of the Lord instructs me to have all of them shout in English: I am a Joseph! (English is their primary language)

They shouted this phrase over and over. I will never forget this amazing meeting where the **Spirit of God was so tangible that you could cut it with a knife**. Now they could not pronounce Joseph the way we do in the USA, so they ended up shouting: **I Am a YOSEPH**! Over and over they shouted: **I Am a YOSEPH**! The whole prison shook as these approximately 40 young men declaring with all of their hearts and vocal abilities by the **Spirit** of the Lord: **I Am a YOSEPH! I Am a YOSEPH! I Am a YOSEPH!** I will never forget that day as long as I live!

Both my son and I began to weep for these young men as the **Spirit** of **God** overwhelmed them. Then my son Daniel and I took every one of those young men one at a time into are arms, shedding tears and praying for them that they would become a Joseph even as they had boldly proclaimed. We all stood there in amazement and tears as **GOD** had stepped down from heaven to be with us at that moment! Here we were in a high-security prison surrounded by the very Presence of **God**, with Heaven come to earth!

They Ran for the Altar Weeping and Wailing

I was ministering in a little country called Suriname, which is located right below Brazil across the Amazon River. A precious brother and pastor from the Baltimore **Christ**ian center had arranged for me to be speaking in small gatherings. In these meetings, a precious apostolic sister by the name of Rinia Refos, heard me speak. The Lord touched her in such a wonderful way that she wanted me to meet her apostle, who is over one of the largest churches in this nation. She took me to this precious Elderly Apostle. I gave her one of my books about my experience of going to hell. And shared with her some of my testimony.

After we had left this meeting, I think approximately a day later sister Rinia Refos informed me that her apostle would love to have me speak at the next Sunday morning service. I agreed to this request. It came into my heart to begin to prepare for this service. I informed my son Daniel and the peoples whose house where I was staying that I would not be eating for a number of days, in order to get the mind of **CHRIST**.

It came into my heart that I was to share from memory the book of James. **God** has allowed me to memorize ten books of the New Testament, including many Scriptures. All I did for approximately three days was quote the book of James over and over to myself slowly, meditating upon its wonderful truths.

Back in 1997, when I had originally memorized this book, I had informed my congregation that I would be sharing it on a Sunday night. That I would be preaching the book of James from beginning to end by memory. I still remember that amazing night. There were hundreds of people who had shown up to hear me proclaim this message. As I was ministering, I could sense **a mighty move of God** beginning to take place. When I gave the altar call well over 100 people (believers) came running for the altar weeping and wailing. **God** did a wonderful work that night!

Here I was once again meditating, praying and pondering, musing upon the book of James. The Sunday morning I was to speak finally came. As I entered the sanctuary, (which I believe sits about 3000), was almost filled. Now in the natural, I'm a little bit nearsighted. This building was narrow and very deep. The stage was about 3 to 4 feet high. The very 1st row of chairs I think was probably about 30 feet away. When I stood upon the stage, I could see the 1st couple of rolls of people, but from there back, it was very blurry.

Now to say that I was pumped up, would not be sufficient to declare how I felt at this moment. I had been fasting and quoting the book of James for three days from morning to night. My heart had been filled with the **FIRE** of heaven. The lady who was to interpret for me stood by the pulpit. Now, this is where I messed up. I was so pumped up that I was standing on the very edge of the stage as if I was trying to get out to the people.

I am sure they were expecting me to stand right there next to the pulpit. The precious lady who was to interpret for me was behind my back. I had a microphone in my hand, waiting to be released upon these precious people with the truths of the book of James burning in my heart. I have a terrible habit of speaking fast as it is, but now I had to have it interpreted in their language. As I began to speak, rapidly, this precious lady kept trying to get me to slow down.

It also seemed to me that the apostle sitting on the front row of chairs was not very happy with what was going on. In my heart, I began to get extremely frustrated with myself because I felt like I was messing up (and I was). As I continued to preach the book of James from my heart, it seems like things were going from bad to worse.

The interpreter kept trying to get me to slow up, and to turn around and speak to where she could see my lips. I knew that my time was running out, and I wanted to get to chapter 3 and chapter 4. As I was speaking, I saw that there was a lot of motion taking place in the congregation. It seemed to me that people did not want to stay in their chairs. I could not see very well because of my nearsightedness.

I finally came to the place where I knew I had run out of time. I finished speaking a little bit out of chapter 3 and chapter 4. I felt as if in my heart that if I did not stop soon, they would drag me off the stage. So, in my heart, with utter defeat, I gave the altar call. During this whole time, there had been movement going on in the congregation. I thought within my mind that they were leaving out of frustration of me speaking so fast and because the interpreter was not being able to interpret what I was saying — w**hat a disaster. Or so I thought**!

When I gave the altar call, something amazing happened. People were running for the front. In a very brief time, the whole front of this large sanctuary was filled with people who were weeping and crying. I began to look for workers, altar workers to help with these precious people who had come forward. But there was nobody to help. I went down into the mist of them trying to pray for as many as I could. This went on for quite a while. Eventually, people began to wander away. In my heart, I was so grateful that these people responded to my terrible message, but I still felt like I was a complete failure.

A number of days went by, as I was ministering in other smaller fellowships. The precious sister who had set up these meetings

(Rinia Refos) while we were in the car, brought up this meeting. She said to me: was it not just amazing how **God** moved in the meeting on Sunday? This statement completely baffled me. I asked her to explain what she meant? I told her because of my nearsightedness, I could not tell what was going on.

She told me that as I began to preach and teach from the book of James that the **power of God had hit the congregation**. That, as I was preaching people, were falling out of their chairs, and being tossed about by the **power of God**. I could hardly believe what I was hearing. I knew I had seen movement, but I did not know that it was the **Holy Ghost** moving. And then she said something that was even more amazing! She told me that it was wonderful that when I gave the altar call and all those people who had come forward. I told her I was blessed with that also, but I asked her where the leaders of the Church were.

That's when she informed me about the most amazing thing about the whole meeting was that all those people who had come running forward weeping and wailing before **God were the leaders of the church**. Yes, it was the leaders of the church that **God** had convicted! For judgment, must 1st begin in the house of the Lord. This is the reason why there was nobody there to help pray for them. Despite my overzealousness, and lack of wisdom **God** had once again shown up to do a mighty work.

If you ever did it once, he'll do it again.

How to Live in the Miraculous!

This is a quick explanation of how to live and move in the realm of the miraculous. Seeing **Divine** interventions of **God** is not something that just spontaneously happens because you have been born-again. There are certain biblical principles and truths that must be evident in your life. This is a very basic list of some of these truths and laws:

1. You must give **JESUS CHRIST** your whole heart. You cannot be lackadaisical in this endeavour. Being lukewarm in your walk with **God** is repulsive to the Lord. He wants 100% commitment. **JESUS** gave him all; now it is our turn to give our all. He loved us 100%. Now we must love Him 100%.

My son, give me thine heart and let thine eyes observe my ways (Proverbs 23:26).

So then because thou art lukewarm, and neither cold nor hot, I will spew thee out of my mouth (Revelation 3:16).

2. There must be a complete agreement with **God**'s Word. We must be in harmony with the Lord in our attitude, actions, thoughts, and deeds. Whatever the Word of **God** declares in the New Testament is what we wholeheartedly agree with.

Can two walk together, except they be agreed? (Amos 3:3).

For the eyes of the LORD run to and fro throughout the whole earth, to shew himself strong in the behalf of them whose heart is perfect toward him (2 Chronicles 16:9).

3. Obey and do the Word from the heart, from the simplest to the most complicated request or command. No matter what the Word says to do, do it! Here are some simple examples: Lift your hands in praise, in everything give thanks, forgive instantly, gather together with the saints, and give offerings to the Lord, and so on.

I can of mine own self do nothing: as I hear, I judge: and my judgment is just; because I seek not mine own will, but the will of the FATHER, which hath sent me (John 5:30).

4. Make **JESUS** the highest priority of your life. Everything you do, do not do it as unto men, but do it as unto **God**.

If ye then be risen with CHRIST, seek those things which are above, where CHRIST sitteth on the right hand of God. Set your affection on things above, not on things on the earth (Colossians 3:1-2).

5. Die to self! The old man says, "My will be done!" The new man says, "**God**'s will be done!"

I am crucified with CHRIST: nevertheless, I live; yet not I, but CHRIST liveth in me: and the life which I now live in the flesh I live by the faith of the Son of God, who loved me, and gave himself for me (Galatians 2:20).

Now if we are dead with CHRIST, we believe that we shall also live with him (Romans 6:8).

6. Repent the minute you get out of **God**'s will—no matter how minor, or small the sin may seem.

(Revelation 3:19).

As many as I love, I rebuke and chasten: be zealous therefore, and repent.

7. Take one step at a time. **God** will test you (not to do evil) to see if you will obey him. *Whatever He tells you to do: by His Word, by His* ***Spirit****, or within your conscience, do it.* He will never tell you to do something contrary to His nature or His Word!

> ***For whosoever shall do the will of my FATHER, which is in heaven, the same is my brother, and sister, and mother (Matthew 12:50).***

ABOUT THE AUTHOR

Michael met and married his wonderful wife (Kathleen) in 1978. As a direct result of the Author and his wife's personal, amazing experiences with God, they have had the privilege to serve as pastors/apostles, missionaries, evangelist, broadcasters, and authors for over four decades.

They have broadcasted the Gospel on their own radio stations. Propagated the Gospel by TV, Satellite and Internet. Owning

their own 24 hour TV network (wbntv.org). Having personally helped start over 27 churches.

Doc has published over 100 books, with many more coming (Lord willing). Pioneered a Bible College, and Christian school. Doc Yeager has thousands of video sermons on the Internet. Having written over 5000 sermon outlines on over 30 different subject matters of the Bible. Preached over 10,000 times.

Having memorized most of the New Testament! Earned a PhD in Biblical Theology, and received a conferred Doctorate of Divinity from Life Christian University.

Their books are filled with literally thousands of their Amazing testimonies of Gods protection, provision, healing's, miracles, and answered prayers.

They flow in the gifts of the Holy Spirit, teaching the word of God, with wonderful signs following and confirming God's word. Websites Connected to Doc Yeager.

www.docyeager.com

www.jilmi.org

www.wbntv.org

Some of the Books Written by Doc Yeager:

"Living in the Realm of the Miraculous – "1 to 5 "
"I need God Cause I'm Stupid"
"The Miracles of Smith Wigglesworth"
"How Faith Comes 28 WAYS"
"Horrors of Hell, Splendors of Heaven"
"The Coming Great Awakening"
"Sinners in The Hands of an Angry GOD",
"Brain Parasite Epidemic"
"My JOURNEY to HELL" - illustrated for teenagers
"Divine Revelation of Jesus Christ"

"My Daily Meditations"
"Holy Bible of JESUS CHRIST"
"War In The Heavenlies - (Chronicles of Micah)"
"My Legal Rights to Witness"
"Why We (MUST) Gather! - 30 Biblical Reasons"
"My Incredible, Supernatural, Divine Experiences"
"How GOD Leads & Guides! - 20 Ways"
"Weapons of Our Warfare"
"How You Can Be Healed"
"Hell Is For Real"
"Heaven Is For Real"
"God Still Heals"
"God Still Provides"
"God Still Protects"
"God Still Gives Dreams & Visions"
"God Still Does Miracles"
"God Still Gives Prophetic Words"
"Life Changing Quotes of Smith Wigglesworth"

Made in the USA
Monee, IL
07 May 2024

58097782R10164